Body Speech

Body
Speech

by Samy Molcho

Translated by Ivanka Roberts

St. Martin's Press
New York

Library of Congress Cataloging in Publication Data

Molcho, Samy.
    Body speech.

    1. Nonverbal communication (Psychology)   2. Success.
I. Title.
BF637.C45M614   1985   153.6   85-1739
ISBN 0-312-08741-1 (pbk.)

10 9 8 7 6 5 4 3 2 1

To my parents who raised me
and enabled me to develop freely,
who did not impose their will on me
and taught me to be independent
and responsible for my own actions.

To my wife, whose love never ties me down,
and enables me to
truly share my feelings with her,
free of my own ego.

Contents

Our First Language

We spend time and energy learning a foreign language in addition to our mother tongue. In the course of time, body language has become a foreign language. We do not have to learn foreign languages, but it is an advantage if we do. We reduce the danger of misunderstandings. I cannot understand why we never have the time to improve our primary language, in other words the language of our body. Since no one can evade or suppress this particular way of communicating—body language—it would be very advantageous to learn it; after all, it provides us with important information about the inner attitudes and leanings of our fellow beings.

If we keep an open mind and watchful eye for the signals and comments of our body language, many conversations and meetings can be carried on much more easily and successfully. Knowledge of body language, the silent question-and-answer game in our bodily behaviour, opens direct paths to other people, and freer relationships with them. In some speechless blinks-of-an-eye we sense this: A glance, a turn of the head, a "touching" gesture, a rejecting motion, says more than a thousand words.

As a child develops, one can observe how the natural behaviour of an infant gradually adapts to the body behaviour expected of him by his family. Because if he does not, he will not be correctly understood within the body language usage of his family. Actually the process is always the same, and usually boils down to similar basic models. The child learns colloquial body language. But depending on the characteristic features of mother, father, brothers, and sisters, and the circumstances in which they live together, there are innumerable individual variations.

Adolescents, too, develop their own codes of body language within their circles, and often express themselves much more precisely and clearly through it than with words. Even their opposition to, and protest against, accepted rules and regulations is expressed much more strongly in body behavior than in speech. One can see this in their casual dealings with one another, as well as in their "demonstrative" behaviour when dealing with adults. Parents, teachers, and politicians then simply declare it to be "bad behaviour," and are infuriated by it. Thus tensions and so-called "generation conflicts" often occur merely because we do not know how to handle these body signals, and we interpret them wrongly. If an adolescent makes a disparaging hand gesture and at the same time briefly shrugs his shoulders, his peers understand it quite simply as a declaration of an objection. His mother or teacher, however, sees it as a contemptuous or aggressive gesture and hits the roof. A misinterpretation turns into a conflict.

Yet the reason for this misunderstanding is easy to see: The body language of the adults follows a different code. Almost all adults have very definite, clear-cut expectations to meet in their job at the company or in the office, as well as in their social role. Different rules of behaviour apply to a factory worker than to a department manager, different ones to a doctor than to a bus driver. These expectations and rules also mold their body language: It is a mirror of their social roles.

Linguists and sociologists speak of a "restricted code," a limited vocabulary and ability to communicate, from which one can recognize the class a person belongs to, and his social status. There is also the "elaborated code": This is used by people who generally come from wealthier families, have had better educational opportunities, and attain a professional position that provides them with—and permits—a rich vocabulary and varied use of language.

These characteristics can also be applied to body language. Admittedly the point is not to recognize a person's profession from his hand movements, as in the television program "What's My Line." But social status, standing, and self-assessment within a group and its structure—the social position of people—can be revealed through their body language.

One can learn the "appropriate" body language, and usually does so unconsciously, throughout one's life. But one thing never changes: Our body language is clearer than the language of words. "One doesn't have complete control of one's body" says a truism. Our body always reacts spontaneously and cannot dissimulate as our words can. The body is primary—not the word.

As an artist I observe this with an intensity which undoubtedly most people do not experience; it merely flashes by them as a confusing phenomenon from time to time. However, good actors—very good ones—develop this ability: Their bodies, and not their brains, shape a character, incorporating its individuality and its habits.

As a mime I study a person and a type, their circumstances and their reactions. I compare them with the knowledge I have acquired and the observations I have made; consider how they apply to this person and this situation. I try to translate these observations into a character again, to form life, personality again out of this reality. What helps is that in contrast to the "original"—the prototype or precedent—I am aware of the flow of my body tension, I know about my nerve signals and the movement of my muscles, and their interaction, and can consciously control them because this is my craft, my trade. Through the language of my body, I make myself into the prototype or representation of this character.

In doing this I achieve an effect that is very natural, but because of our ignorance of the character of the signal and the feedback effect of bodily posture, it seems remarkable. I, the mime, become the image of this person, as well as being myself. I do not merely imitate the singular gestures and motions of this character. I also reconstruct this person's thoughts, feelings, and

One can become aware of body language and its signals. To do this, one must be critical of oneself, and tolerant toward others.

12

emotions. In conscious assessment of his characteristics I control his muscle reactions through brain and nerve cells, and then am myself confirmed or refuted in my bodily identity through the feedback of information from these sense organs. Through the experiences and reactions of my own body I learn about the dependencies and nuances of human behaviour more explicitly, more convincingly and accurately, than through information from and observation of the outside world.

While teaching at the Vienna Academy of Music and Performing Arts at the Max Reinhardt Seminar, and particularly in manager-training courses about the importance of body

Four Humours

Samy Molcho as

A choleric   *A melancholic*

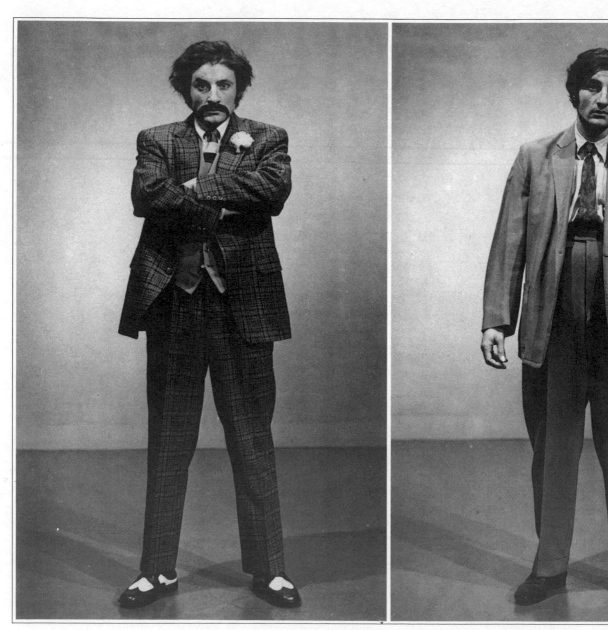

language, I have often heard the question: What's it good for, and how can it be used?

This is easy to explain to an actor, because it is one of the tools of his trade. Young people, at least if they have sensitive perception in addition to intellectual commitment, grasp my answer just as quickly: It is a way of understanding oneself and others better.

Yet they rightly and disapprovingly ask: What are you doing, Samy Molcho, you, a well-known artist, with your reputation and your knowledge, putting yourself at the disposal of tycoons—so that they can better condition their subordinates

A phlegmatic   A sanguine person

A professor of transcendental logic

and customers?! My answer is: No, emphatically no! They—the students—are meant to understand others better, and that first means that they have to learn the language of their own bodies. Through this act one becomes more humble, and hopefully more tolerant.

I would like to illustrate this with a conversation from one such seminar for managers. First, of course, comes the question: How should *I* behave correctly, how can I manipulate *others* better; what guidelines do you have to offer, what guarantee of success? My answer: I have no set formulas. Neither for success in business, nor for advancement professionally or socially, nor for personal rapport or individual harmony. Yet I am convinced that we can make our life more understandable for ourselves and more comprehensible to others

A model citizen

if we learn to pay attention to our own body signals and those of others. In doing this, of course, there is a tremendously negative possibility, a danger: to use the expansion of our knowledge of each other to expand our own power, and for social manipulation.

I believe the expansion of our knowledge is firstly always a benefit, and free of moral judgements. After that, well, it always depends on what one is looking for. Through body language I try to understand myself and others better, and to find more human closeness. There are no prescriptions for this. One has to learn this anew with every partner, every person one deals with. I would like to help you understand their signals better and to answer them more openly.

Because we human beings always have two levels of

communication. One is verbal: We communicate the substance of a piece of information through the spoken word. The second level is nonverbal: body language. We seldom express the subjective experience of a conversation and the feelings and attitudes connected with this information in words—but they are recognizable in our body behaviour through specific signals. It is important to correctly understand *both* levels of communication, because often important additional information remains unspoken, or possibly there is even a contradiction between what is said and what is meant, which causes confusion and misunderstanding. I can illustrate this with two examples.

A child would like to go and play. His mother says, "Of course, my darling!" and bends down to him, hugs him, gives him a kiss, and pushes him toward the coat closet with a smile. The little boy knows: Mother is happy to let me play. She is showing me that I should take care, and is reminding me to put on my jacket.

The same situation, and the answer, "Of course you can go and play!" And while the mother is saying this, she raises her shoulders (defencive posture), drops them again (sign of resignation), pulls her head back, and her mouth and face express disapproval. Which information should the child react to? And how will the little boy feel when he goes out to play?

There is an obvious contradiction here, and even the little boy can recognize it relatively easily. However, unfortunately there are many signals that one does not register immediately, which one must first make oneself aware of. Yet one still reacts to them, because the body is incapable of not communicating. Then, however, tensions and inhibitions develop, even while their source remains hidden.

Every person acts as a stimulus or a reflex on his surroundings through his posture and behaviour. Others react to it positively or indifferently. But whatever the case, there is a retroaction, a feedback. We can also see this in our own reactions. That is yet another reason to pay attention to the stimuli that we ourselves send out.

After all, quite often we say that someone is aggressive or conceited, because that is what we feel he is. Yet at the same time we know from others, or through our own observations, that this person has a sense of humour, can be very loving, is to be trusted. In this case, should not the first question be: Could I be at fault? Maybe I am sending out stimuli that make him react aggressively toward me? To what extent do the people around me see me as I think they do?

Naturally each one of us believes that he or she

behaves agreeably and considerately toward the person he or she is with. Yet one time the response will be reserved, the next time it will be aggressive. So do I really behave agreeably, or do I trigger the aggressiveness through my behaviour? Since we do not consciously register our customary behaviour, we normally do not perceive this feedback effect for what it is. We say it is the other person who behaves like that, and we do not realize that the cause lies with us. That is why I say: Change your attitude toward other people, and they will change their attitude toward you.

Showtime

18

The human being is a complex of desires and contradictions. One has to view this as a whole in order to understand him. This also applies to the language of his body: One may not interpret individual parts, since only the whole body gives us the picture. Here comes a man toward me with totally open posture and a frank look—I almost expect him to embrace me. And then he gives me—no, he surrenders to me—a hand that does not respond to the touch of mine, it just lies in my palm quite passively. The interaction of these signals tells

The crooner

me: Though this man is attentive toward me, he sets great store on keeping his distance, and will not actually allow himself to be "touched."

Body signals can also have multiple interpretations. It depends on who receives them and what the recipient's interest is concentrated on. A smile is a friendly signal. If a reserved woman between two suitors eventually smiles at one of them, it is a signal of consent for him, and a sign of rejection for his rival. If she simultaneously places her hand on the rival's arm, she reverses this interpretation; she is now acting ambiguously. And apart from that, the young woman is a flirt, and calculating. In other words, one always has to gather all the facts in a given situation, and interpret them correctly.

I just hope that in doing this, the same thing will not happen to any of us as happened to the professor who was experimenting with a flea. He tore off one of its legs, and called, "Jump!" and the flea jumped. So he entered that fact in his notebook. The same happened with the second, third, and fourth leg. Then it was time for the next one.

But the flea did not react to his command. The scholar concluded: "When one tears off a flea's fifth leg, it goes deaf."

My object is to improve communication between people. I believe that we can live together in harmony—within the family and on the job, in social circles and with business contacts. Therefore we have to learn to deal with one another in such a way as to assure satisfaction and self-awareness on both sides. All competitive behaviour that orients itself according to the offending and injurious aims "victor and loser" is worse than the cheapest Wild West stereotype. At least in those, one knows that the victor is always noble and the loser a villain. In life it is usually different, and the victims more numerous. "One can win oneself to death" states a wise adage that is worth bearing in mind. In a Western it is the hero who rides off alone across the prairie. He leaves the urban community. Where will we find new partners, friends, customers in this life if we have killed them all with our superiority, and antagonized them with our aggression?

Each of us wants to be noticed and respected. Respect means recognition; literally it is "looking back," returning a glance. Noticing means, first of all, recognizing body signals and behaviour. Communicating means interpreting those signals correctly and answering intelligibly. One needs one's head for that, but communication also comes from the heart—the signal, as well as the body's answer.

The Body Is the Glove of the Soul

I do not believe in the dualism of body and soul. They are inseparable. We merely have to ask ourselves one simple question: Do I have a body, or am I my body? As far as I am concerned, the answer is clear: As long as I am alive, and actively communicate with others, I am my body. The English language has clear-cut terms for this identity. "Some*body*" is someone, "no*body*" is no one. Without a body, there is no life, and no concept of ourselves.

No, I do not want to raise any theological controversies, not to mention issues of faith. It is up to each individual to decide how to shape his faith, his views of life and death.

I am speaking of something that can be proved, can be experienced—my body. And it strikes me that many religions do not promise us paradise until after we are dead. Is that meant to mean that we cannot find fulfillment during our life here on earth? That we have to suffer as long as we are bodies? One speaks of the "sins of the flesh," "carnal appetites"; everything that satisfies the desires of our body seems threatened by the curse of depravity, right down to original sin. Is this not the reason for our negative attitude to our body and to life? Is this not a cause of our difficulties in accepting our body and living freely and self-confidently in our corporeality? When we are in danger, we call out: "Save our souls"—yet what we really mean is save our bodies, so we can go on living. Only in religion and poetry can our body be separated from our soul.

Yet even here the profoundest symbols and most moving images cannot be separated from bodily expression. The Body of Christ is one such example with profound significance. Or the German poet Hoelderlin's hymnal declaration: "Oh Holy heart of nations, Oh Motherland!"

Or Joseph von Eichendorff's nostalgic verse: "And my soul spread wide its wings, soared o'er the silent land, as if t'were flying home."

Perception and reality, life and soul, are almost inseparable in human imagination.

The body is the glove of the soul: to be handled with sensitivity and acute awareness.

What we are, we are through our bodies. Our body is the glove of our soul, its language the words of our heart. All inner sentiments, feelings, emotions, desires are expressed by our body. What we call body expression is the expression of inner emotions.

We are aware of ourselves and our environment only through our body. The nervous system and sense organs transmit these perceptions to the brain as stimuli, and there they are registered in two ways: firstly as a phenomenon, secondly as pleasant or unpleasant. We have no other kind of perception, and therefore we first have to explain how this organism—the body—functions, so that we can also understand how it reacts. Only a thorough understanding of our organism's system makes it possible for us to comprehend the building blocks of our body language.

The Construction Plan of the Organism

The human organism is created through the interaction of two elements: energy and genetic information. We use the initials ATP to denote the energy storage. When nutrients are broken down, energy is set free which is used to produce adenosine triphosphate (ATP). The energy contained in this phosphate bond is at the body cells' disposal for their work and can either be used to synthesize cellular components or be converted into other forms of energy—for instance, to move (contract) muscles. This organic "power station" is a miracle in itself.

We know the information storage as DNA—that is the abbreviation for deoxyribonucleic acid. It is contained in the chromosomes of each cell; genes are made of it. The molecules of DNA are bound in the form of a double spiral (double helix) and contain the entire construction plan of our organism and all necessary information for self-preservation. These nucleic acid chains have up to two billion codes in humans! The DNA molecule divides into two halves, and each of these halves restores itself again, using free nucleotides, into exactly the same sequence. Identical replication is the name we give to this fantastic ability to reproduce exactly the same information in exactly the same sequence over millions of generations of cells. Every single one of our hundreds of trillions of body cells contains the total genetic code, the entire operating instructions of our organism. And through the genes with their forty-six chromosomes we transmit this code: Twenty-three paternal, twenty-three maternal chromosomes unite to form the genetic pattern of the child. The uniqueness of our organism is determined by this genetic information, and thus our individuality is shaped. According to the laws of its unique provisions, it regulates growth and development, the qualities that stimulate our needs and determine our individuality.

These, then, are the basic components of our organic system. Let us now look at how our body works, how it reacts and acts.

The nervous system serves the purpose of receiving and transmitting messages. This is done through chemical reactions and electrical impulses. The centre which receives all the messages and transmits the commands is our brain. The brain responds by sending signals, which make the organism aware of necessities and needs. You are thirsty, so you have to drink. You are afraid and wish to run away. For these responses the brain in its turn activates chemical and motor actions. The nervous system can be divided into two groups according to these functions:

- One group receives messages through the sense organs.
- The other group gives motor impulses, which we perceive as muscle movements.

But that cannot be all, you could now object. A person breathes without thinking about it. Our digestion functions. Our blood circulates. The brain surely has nothing to do with that. Hold on!

Biocybernetics—this is a comparative science, which explores the regulating and control processes in organic systems—has discovered that in the human organism, too, processes take place that are well known to us from technological systems. For it talks about a "closed system" and an "open system" that regulate and control the functions of our body.

In the closed system, constant desired values are established and their observance is automatically regulated. This includes a "feeler," which measures the actual value, a "regulator," which compares the actual value with the desired value, and a "control element," which corrects the deviation from the desired value. The feeler announces the present state to the regulator, which brings the control element to rest when the actual value is attained. Each of us is familiar with this regulatory mechanism in the closed system from our heating thermostat. You set the desired temperature at 70°F, the desired value. Everything else happens without our further involvement: The thermostat "feels" the actual value, which is compared with the desired value, and if the temperature is too low, the burner is activated by a control element, and not turned off until the thermostat announces that the actual value and desired value correspond again, and the temperature of 70°F has been reached.

Our body regulates its temperature according to the same principle. It is not the temperature of the skin that is decisive, but the temperature of the blood—we can measure it with a thermometer. The lowest necessary desired value is 97.7°F. If the temperature rises above this—the body is overheated, is reacting to a sickness with a fever—a cooling process is automatically set in motion. We begin to perspire and the dampness that develops on the surface of our skin is designed to lower the body temperature through evaporation. If, on the other hand, our temperature drops, and we start to freeze, our body begins to shiver. This generates heat. Whether this reaction is always sufficient to restore the normal condition of

Advances-Rejection (left to right)

She meets his appraising glance with coy flirtation. Hands and arms shield her genital area.

His disinterest is expressed by the way he carries his chest. His hands protect his genitals. She reacts by turning away.

His flirtatious "well-behaved sitting posture" attracts her attention.

His withdrawal is triggered by her aggressive threatening gesture: While she flirts with him, her toe points at his abdomen.

His right hand signals possessiveness; simultaneously his left elbow wards off possible rivals.

She happily accepts being "handled" by him.

97.7°F is another question. Until it does succeed, our organism is in danger.

The crucial point is that our body reacts instantly to the difference between desired value and actual value, without our conscious intervention. More than that: We cannot consciously influence the closed circle of this regulatory system. Nature does not rely on human consciousness. If we try to interfere with this system by, for instance, holding our breath or suppressing excretion, we do not succeed. We faint, the conscious is thus turned off, and the organism functions autonomously, supplies the lungs with oxygen, and we breathe. And in the other case we inevitably dirty our pants at some point.

A further refinement is built into this regulatory system. It functions according to priorities, their sequence determined by the primary vital necessities of the situation at that time. We can do nothing about it. If we find ourselves in the middle of a fire, we want to run away as quickly as possible. But because of panic and exertion our body has difficulty in breathing. Despite our consciousness of the danger, we are forced to stop and correct our breathing difficulty—the deviation of the actual value from the desired value.

These examples show how little influence we have on controlling the closed regulatory system. It is true that with a great deal of effort and concentration we are able to affect some things; for instance we can slow down our breathing, or stabilize our circulation through self-hypnosis. However, these are minimal changes. Everything vital to the proper functioning of our organism is determined by the closed system.

The open system is a different matter altogether. Here we control the behaviour of our body through more or less conscious processes. The brain sets the desired values, the object of our behaviour. Sensitive nerve cells and the sense organs (the ''feelers'') perceive internal and external stimuli and conduct them to the brain via the sensory nerves. There the actual value and the desired value are compared, and corrective commands are given to the muscles via the motor nerve tracts, which then carry out the appropriate movements. The whole body functions as an instrument of our will. Information is of vital importance in this. Only when the actual value is reported very quickly and accurately can the regulator, the brain, steer its control element, the body, toward the intended desired value.

This can be graphically illustrated by a simple comparison. Our brain operates like the captain of a ship. He plans his route, which is the desired value. He receives the actual values via various feelers, and determines his course and steers his ship according to them: distance and measurement, currents and speed, direction and expended power of the engines. Suddenly one feeler, the sonar, sends him the message: "Reef ahead!" He gives the command, "To port!" and while his ship steers around the rocks, he continually checks the sonar range findings in order to keep the deviation from the course as small as possible, and to be able to turn back toward his destination as soon as possible.

Everyone else on the ship would spontaneously protest: "Why are you veering left, our destination lies straight ahead!" Optically his decision seems to be wrong—and yet it is correct. The captain merely received more information and utilized all values at his disposal in order to find the correct conduct, which alone will lead to his destination. If he had obstinately stuck to his desired value, or had ignored or not received all the information, the ship would inevitably have collided with the reef.

The same happens in every society, every business, every family. A goal is set, and a plan to achieve it. Then information comes in which makes the direct route to the goal impossible. The plans have to be changed, the course corrected, in order to reach the same goal. If the citizens ignore these actual values, if the coworkers are too inflexible to make the correction, if the members of the family cling to their fantasies (desired values)—conflict becomes unavoidable and disaster possible.

But we should return to our body behaviour and illustrate with a very simple example what this open regulatory system is able to accomplish. I want to pick up a glass without looking at it. My hand misses it. So I use my eyes to help me. They signal: Too far to the right, and the brain gives the command: farther to the left. Or vice versa, until my hand reaches the glass. But I still do not have it in my hand, because the command has not been given: Close your fingers around it. Maybe it is given too soon because we turn our eyes away at that moment. Then our actual value is missing, and our grasp goes wide.

This example seems to be very disjointed—but that is exactly how the whole thing proceeds! With an electronic stop-action camera that photographs each phase of the movement, one can see that the hand really does constantly correct its course until it grasps the glass.

In my opinion it is very important for us to become aware of this constant checking and correcting in all our movements. Because only then will we really get to know our body and know how to deal with it. And it is also fun, enjoyable, to pursue and further develop this wonderful kind of interaction. This process of comparison and conversion gives a fascination and form to many games. It can be seen most clearly in golf, where it has become a regular ritual involving an extreme degree of body control.

Look at a golfer. His aim is to hit a hard rubber ball with a diameter of one and five-eighths inches as straight as possible into a four-and-a-half-inch hole, over a distance of 220 to 550 yards, using ten or twelve finely graduated clubs. Drive, approach shot, putt. That in itself is a perfect parable for the tuning mechanism of an open regulatory system. And once again, everything depends on correctly receiving and utilizing information. Distance, wind conditions, state of the turf—right down to the cut of the grass on the close-cropped green. The more accurately the actual values are registered, the more precise are the brain's instructions and the demands on the body's movements, so that they are transmitted to the instruments—the clubs and the ball—and lead to the desired value: the hole.

Relationships between people follow comparable rules of drawing closer to each other, whether it is at home or at work. One has a purpose to a conversation, one is seeking consensus. That is the desired value, the hole. Now we examine the circumstances and atmosphere of our meeting, what is said, the mimicry, the posture of the person we are with, and the constant shifting of these actual values. We adjust our arguments, our facial and our body expression; we react so as to arrive at our goal despite the divergent components.

I believe that we generally assess our options relatively realistically. Experience has taught us not to aim too high. And just in case we do not achieve the desired value, we often prepare a backup position, an alternative aim, with which we are willing to be satisfied. Yet we often cannot achieve that, either. And I wonder: Could it be because we have not correctly dealt with our information? Maybe we did not receive all the important information, or have wrongly interpreted it, or even answered it with inconsistent information?

What Does "Information" Actually Mean?

We have talked about the construction plan of the organism. About its energy storage (ATP) from which it gets its strength, and about the information storage (DNA) in which its characteristics are fixed down to the smallest detail. We talked

about the closed system with which the body regulates its unconscious autonomic functions, and about the open system with which we control conscious processes and movements.

    I am sure that some of you have noticed that I repeatedly use terms that one does not expect to find in a book about body language: communication and information, storage, transmission, utilization, and feedback. One is more likely to expect such technical terms in a book about telecommunications or automatic control processes. Yet this very association of thoughts is absolutely correct: Our body, every organism, is among other things a magnificently organized communications network. Of course, this ability is considerably more developed in a human being than in an insect or an amoeba. But all organic life—even a plant—is capable of living only to the extent and in the manner to which its communication network is developed and functions. Since this is considerably more complex and complicated in a human, a thinking being, he also receives different information more discriminatingly than other living creatures.

    What, actually, is information? Something new? Not at

Selection: General information is blocked, usable information is purposefully noted.

all. The world is full of bits of information, they are always present and we are defenceless against their abundance. They are new only to the person who perceives them for the first time. Otherwise they are facts, conditions, events. This means a piece of information is anything that we receive from the world in us or around us through our sensitive and sensory organs.

We are very selective about it. We choose only what we need, or think we need, from the abundance of possible information. This depends on our desired values. We seek and compare the actual values that are important for our body functions or the goals we have set. Thus they become information. Through our senses they reach our central nervous system (brain and spinal cord), where they are registered, sorted, and stored. The result of these impressions and perceptions is what we experience.

The purpose of storage is, of course, to be able to react to the collected information. Via the motor nerve tracts it is converted into movements and actions that serve to satisfy our needs, desires, and interests—in other words, to adjust the actual values to the desired values. We collect information that is useful to us—anything else would be absurd. Its storage even follows an order of preference determined by several criteria.

The first is frequency. The more often an experience repeats itself, the more firmly it imprints itself. Through corrections and repetition we develop the best means to respond to it. The reaction to certain situations becomes programmed. For instance our body knows "blindly" how to walk up the stairs from the first to the second floor of our house. If, after being repaired, just one step is different, we are thrown off balance. Our body corrects its program, until even this knowledge registers only in the subconscious.

Another criterion of order of preference is the intensity of an experience. Your first great love, a fabulous evening at the theatre, a heart attack—all these things leave a deep impression. We can gather factual information—for instance, about investing in a house—bit by bit, as partial information. An experience has various degrees of intensity, but it is always a whole. There are no partial experiences—any more than there are partial holes.

A further criterion is transience. We and our environment are subjected to a constant dynamic process of change, and our organism has to adapt to it. The adaptive function is included in its program. There is some current information that is associated with constantly changing conditions, and is entered only temporarily into our storage. I am driving along a familiar street, but how I determine speed, lane, and the way I drive depends on the density of the traffic, the lighting, and road conditions. Each time I will drive differently; my brain does not codify a driving program, but operates with current information. It can be compared to entries in our appointment and address book: Names and numbers that we need repeatedly we enter permanently at the back; we throw away the appointments and notes once they have been dealt with. Or if we transfer them, it is because they can be of further use, aid our memory, improve our understanding.

With such notes we reenact what our brain does continually through its ability to store and compare. If some previous information is repeated, encounters a corresponding experience in storage, and thus recognizes the trigger factor (e.g., a hot stove), we talk of "understanding." I understand why I got burned—or why someone behaves one way and not another.

Recognizing an experience makes it easier for us to come to terms with a situation, because we have tested the effect of our reaction and can neither make use of it nor improve it. An example.

When a person is agitated, the rhythm of his heart and breathing accelerates. Awareness of the secondary phenomenon, of the severe pounding of his heart, triggers panic because of the unknown consequences of such a state, and reinforces the existing agitation.

If the person experiences this a second time—the connection of agitation and a pounding heart to panic—he will know that one is dependent on the other and disappears with the cause of the agitation. The reinforcing, unknown quantity is eliminated by experience; panic is now unnecessary. He can concentrate on the cause of the agitation and deal with it through appropriate reactions. This decision is also preceded by a process of selection and establishing priorities.

In order to be able to become aware of its surroundings according to its needs, the human organism must develop the necessary means to do so. Very simple forms of life have very simple programs, and possibly just two data are sufficient for them to react and exist. An insect already has a highly refined faculty of perception, but it still "sees" two-dimensionally. A bee will buzz against a pane of glass again and again, because according to its information something transparent must also be penetrable.

We perceive space three-dimensionally. But in fact this three-dimensional vision is not enough by far to always identify all objects familiar to us, because with every movement—by us or by them—they change their form. Actually we continually see a different object. A cat that curls up, stretches, pounces—all these are entirely different perceptions. It is through the ability to compare and associate stored data that we establish the connections between form and perception. Then that green bundle of fur over there becomes a yellow cat in a blue neon light. We collect and sort impressions and perceptions, compare this information with the stored data, and *this* forms our picture of reality.

Early Stimuli

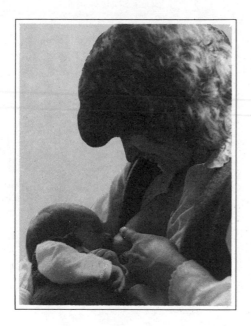

In this section we will discuss development in early childhood and in particular which impulses affect a baby and how it reacts to them.

When does awareness begin? With our birth? Today we know it is even earlier, in the womb. The baby growing in the amniotic sac actually has no problems that could stimulate its senses. It constantly receives its nourishment through a direct conduit, the umbilical cord. Its skin is pleasantly enveloped by the amniotic fluid. Its eyes do not receive any impressions of light. And yet a stimulus from outside itself penetrates through to it: It hears its mother's heartbeat. This is its first reference point and a sign of recognition that shapes its behaviour. This has been documented in clinics through impressive experiments.

Recordings of the mother's heartbeat were played over loudspeakers to screaming and crying babies. They reacted in interestingly different ways. Those newborn babies who had emotional problems due to loss of orientation, and who longed for attention, tenderness, and love, calmed down immediately. However, babies with unfulfilled physical needs—they were hungry, wet, or in pain—continued to scream. This could have a very practical value in the future for care in nurseries: It would be easier to determine which babies have physical needs and which long for emotional reassurance.

Of course a question arises immediately: Are the children focused on the heartbeat of their own mother, or do they simply react to the rhythm of a heart? There is some mollification from the sound of the heartbeat, but the direct effect of their own mother's heart is more convincing. This shows that from the earliest stages we do not have a general conception of ourselves, but a distinct individuality. Every mother has a different heartbeat, and her child orients itself by it. At least in the first stages this particular rhythm is also the link, the communication between mother and child: The newborn baby receives it as a sign of recognition.

This early impression has repercussions much later. We feel comfortable with a certain person, in harmony so to speak, and uncomfortable with another. The one is related to us through the rhythm he emits, the other is strange, different.

A further example: For the vast majority of people, a rocking chair has a magical attraction. If you put one in your room, you will see that almost every guest at some time will head for it, sit down with a smile, and begin to rock. And if you watch closely, you will see that everyone has his own comfortable rhythm.

But have you ever considered that this movement could be determined by a fundamental orientation?

During pregnancy women get accustomed to walking in a certain way, and this tends to become more and more rhythmical as they grow bigger. The unborn child rocks in the amniotic fluid in this same rhythm. It gets used to it, and desires this regular familiar movement even after birth. The mother reacts to this. She almost always holds the baby on her left arm, with his head close to her heart, and gently rocks him. Grandmother will pick him up, rock him, and soothe him in exactly the same way, and the babysitter next door knows equally well that she can get her charge to go to sleep by gently, regularly rocking the cradle. It is always the same basic rhythm of the walk, but just as the mother's steps are varied, so there are definite variations for the baby. We know when we have found the right one, because the crying stops, the breathing becomes regular, and the eyelids droop.

There is a direct relationship between the rhythm of the rocking and breathing. Old people like to use the stimulating effect of the rocking chair, probably unconsciously. Because when one leans back the body opens up, the diaphragm stretches, and one breathes in; and when bending forward, one breathes out with the slight collapse of the upper body.

The soothing rhythm of the heart and walk are constant stimuli to the child in the womb. With birth, an abundance of impressions assault its inexperienced senses. Light, noise, dryness of the skin, hunger. The stomach contracts, the gastric juices start to function. The body is confused by the flood of irritations, the first breaths falter, and in an act of resistance, which is discharged in a scream, the body finds release.

One theory of behavioural science claims that a baby's scream compels the mother to come to him, because the sound could also attract the attention of possible enemies. But to begin with, it is surely simply a bodily reaction; later it becomes a

34

signal, because the mother responds by putting the baby to her breast and satisfying the baby's need for warmth and his hunger. (The sucking motion is, like the movement of a hand that grasps and closes, a natural reflex.) The screaming turns into a signal because the child makes a discovery: His mother comes regularly. If this is not the case, if she reacts arbitrarily or irregularly, she disrupts this feedback system, the normal hunger scream turns into an agitated fear scream, expressing loss of orientation and panic. This connection with the expectations shows clearly how important it is that the interval between the baby's scream and the mother's response be a consistent one. The child has to be able to depend on it, otherwise persistent insecurity and distress result. First experiences leave an indelible impression.

To begin with, the newborn child perceives himself and his surroundings in a very elementary and limited way. The information streaming in to him through his senses is not converted into reactions, because the child does not yet have

Emotions are expressed by spontaneous body movements.

control of his muscles. But this information does trigger an *intention movement,* which can be seen in the change of body tension, the so-called muscle tone. Depending on the intensity of the stimulus, this state of experiencing will be felt by the baby to be pleasant or unpleasant, and will be registered as such in the brain. This is the beginning of the learning process. The pragmatic values are assigned to the information storage of the innate system, through organization and coordination. Gradually the faculty of perception and discernment grows through the repetition of events and impressions; the child learns how to get in contact with the functions and actions of his body.

In this case we make a distinction between spontaneous *"emotion movements"* and practical *"action movements."* If a child stretches out his hand to grasp a temptingly flickering candle flame, it is a purposeful action movement. If he pulls back his hand with a scream, grimaces, and starts to cry, these are emotion movements. They have two effects: First, through them the body becomes conditioned to

The intent stare

getting used to specific reactions; second, they serve as a communication signal.

A newborn child cannot yet show psychic reactions. This ability has to be acquired, because psychic reactions are preceded by repeated experiences and encounters, impressions, associations, repressions, ideals, to which appropriate responses

The instinct to suck is innate in humans. Sucking gives pleasure and stimulates the pleasure senses. If something tastes good, we put it in our mouths.

are formed in our mimicry and gestures. First the child has to develop the organization of such impressions and images in his centre of activity—his brain—and then to learn to control it consciously or unconsciously. Only then can one speak of psychic reactions, a meaningful smile or intentional reserve.

On the other hand, two different childish behavioural patterns will accompany us throughout our lives as expressions of our psychic state. A baby sucks, drinks, smacks his lips, uses his tongue to lick up the last remnants of food in his mouth—that's wonderful! These gestures of pleasure around the mouth appear again and again when we like something, when something tastes good. And when a baby has had enough, he pushes the feeding breast, the nipple of the bottle, or the pacifier out with his tongue. This gesture of refusal will also remain and return as a secondary movement in conflict situations and confrontations.

The finger in the little girl's mouth satisfies an immediate need for pleasure. However, the gesture can also be associated with a pleasurable perception, which in this way is unconsciously transformed into a sensory perception.

Stimuli and Values

With every intense stimulus that hits us hard, our muscles contract. If we receive gentle stimuli that affect us pleasantly, the muscles lengthen. So before we can talk about values, good or bad, we first have to establish something: A stimulus can be more, or less, intense. This has nothing at all to do with a good or bad sensation or experience.

Judgements like good or bad are generally made according to standards that meet social concepts of value and constitute their moral standards. But to begin with, the judgements of our body are subjective and result from its experiences. Does an intense stimulus have a positive or negative effect? It can be either.

The act of love is the result of a very intense stimulating effect. The muscles contract and relax again in order to enjoy the stimulus again, repeated contraction and renewed opening up. This alternation of muscle movements excites us. Our blood is stimulated, our pulse rate increases, the resulting pressure of energy is released in orgasm. If someone does not react to such strong stimuli, we say he or she is cold-blooded, frigid, and deplore the fact that the person does not experience what we find to be extremely positive.

If someone drops an ice cube down our collar, and the cold cube slithers down our back, an intense stimulus is also generated, and a similarly intense reaction. The back of our body closes up (we draw our shoulder blades together), and opens up on the other side (our rib cage expands). Whether one feels this to be pleasant or unpleasant depends on various things, not least on temperature and secondary associations. Your shirt will get wet. A wet shirt is "bad," an ice pack on a feverish brow is "good." But as far as our body is concerned, they are equally strong cold stimuli and it reacts the same way in both cases, by closing and opening the muscles.

These two reactions, *closing* (contraction) and *opening* are the foundation stones of our body language. We recognize tensing and relaxing in their signals. But why do our muscles contract at all? I would like to point out two reasons.

The first is in the nature of the organic system. Closing and contraction could be interpreted as self-defence against constant exposure to stimuli, or as comfort. Simple experiments with electrical impulses have shown that if someone is quite relaxed he reacts to the slightest electrical shock. As soon as he tenses up, the intensity of the impulse has to be increased. With each cramp the flow of information between the nerve's acceptance point and the brain centre is reduced: It is as if we were setting up blocks.

The muscles contract, the body tenses up and thus reduces or blocks receptivity.

Anyone can reenact this process. If you run your hand quite lightly over the surface of a table or a cloth, if you stroke it, you find out a lot about its structure, you feel its fine fibres and little hairs. The information flows through your hand. As soon as you tense your hand, you feel none of these subtleties anymore—at most you feel the place where the table ends or the transition from a piece of fabric to another material. You find limitations, your own and others'. But beyond this, the exchange of information is blocked.

The same applies to human communication. If someone is relaxed, he receives information more easily and accurately; if he is tense, this happens very slowly and disjointedly. We then say that someone is open-minded or closed-minded. But we should not let it rest at this statement. There are innumerable reasons for such tensing up—fear of authority or pressure to achieve, tiredness or exhaustion. As soon as we notice that the person we are talking to has tensed up, we should no longer assume that he is receptive to our information. It would be better to take a break or to postpone the appointment to another day.

The second reason for involuntary muscle contractions is biologically programmed: an escape reaction. If something unpleasant occurs, the obvious behavioural pattern is escape. Things could get dangerous, so one runs away while one still has the chance. It is not until after this intentional reaction that reasons may be developed why one should stay and face the threat after all. But to begin with there is the strong stimulus and the response: escape. Every sudden change in our environment, every abrupt movement, every unexpected noise causes the same reaction. This is just as valid for our emotional behaviour: everything new and unfamiliar is alarming and dangerous to begin with, and we retreat. And it is not only humans who react this way.

If we give a cat some new food, it approaches its familiar bowl. Sniffs: a new smell! A couple of jumps to one side. Then it stops. Second reaction: new, but not bad! The second time it approaches, the olfactory experience is confirmed. The animal pokes its tongue into the bowl: a new taste! Again it retreats, considers: new, and not pleasant! The cat turns away. Or: new, but pleasant! It returns and eats. A completely normal regulatory process in its various stages.

A human being behaves in very much the same way. We first retreat or shut ourselves off from an unfamiliar stimulus. Then we consider the stimulus using stored pragmatic values and accordingly react positively or negatively. One cannot expect someone to open himself up immediately to a new encounter. It is contrary to his nature. There is, admittedly, one exception: if it is linked to a status symbol. Take Malossol caviar—a person who finds it repulsive suppresses his reaction to the best of his ability, and violates his nature with an appreciative smile. A masochist.

But even if someone is a masochist, his body reacts by contracting the muscles when the doctor gets ready to give an injection, because the needle puncture hurts. This example also shows another effect. There are body reactions that are not triggered by the direct stimulus, but originate from associations. Since we assume that the needle puncture will hurt, we prepare our body to flinch. But in the meantime the clever doctor has already given us the shot, and we did not even notice. Or we flinch, although he does not do anything at all.

These kinds of "secondary phenomena" can be seen better in another comparison. We bite into a lemon. Our facial muscles contract, the back of our neck stiffens, our shoulders tense up—all forms of resistance. Our whole upper body withdraws, as if it wanted to run away. Such gestures seem to reduce the extremely strong information, "sour taste," to our brain. Our muscles relax when the stimulus eases off. The body uses analogous forms of expression with thoughts. Someone talks utter rubbish, or submits an impossible proposal, "so that one is left with a sour taste in one's mouth." Then—if one can afford to do it, and does not have to suppress this impulse out of politeness or because of inferior status!—face and shoulders will have the same expression as if one had bitten into a lemon. And anyone watching us immediately understands this body comment, because he himself follows the same code of reactions.

People from all social strata and cultural circles react and act similarly or analogously on the first level of body signals. Nor do these biological primary and secondary phenomena have anything to do with imitation. A deaf-mute, blind child in the Sahel zone will react in exactly the same way to a lemon as a healthy child of its age in America or a street urchin in Lima. It is not a question of learned or acquired behaviour, but a biological

The facial, neck, and shoulder muscles react simultaneously by tensing up when we are affected by a sour experience.

42

reaction that is anchored in the genetic program.

Unpleasant experiences trigger an escape reaction or muscle block. By the second or third time, if not the first, we have learned to attribute them back to physical causes. The very perception of this object, smell, or sound, or this particular situation, is now a warning signal to us. In this way we avoid repeating the experience, which would presumably be equally unpleasant. However practical this regulatory mechanism seems to be, it also conceals a source of error that can lead to incorrect behaviour.

We have bitten into three green apples and each time they were sour. When we come to the fourth one, our warning light goes on and signals: Careful, sour, it will be unpleasant. And we leave it alone. But this apple happens to be sweet and tastes good. We have deprived ourselves of a pleasant experience, because we reacted on an assumption; one piece of information has slipped from our grasp because we did not check the actual value.

The block caused by previous experiences can be advantageous and save us time and trouble, but it also brings with it the danger of misconceptions due to preconceptions. Logically this leads to a way of life in which one files everything that seems to be the same into the same pigeonhole, and establishes the mistaken belief that nothing in life changes. This is convenient, but wrong. Preconceptions are a simplification and solidification of our value judgements, good and bad, which lead to incorrect behaviour due to impeded perception.

We cannot avoid constantly reexamining everything, even at the risk of being disappointed. You meet someone and say to yourself, I know his type, and you dismiss him, do not give him a chance. Someone makes you a proposal. You say to yourself, I know his kind of company, and file the proposal away. Perhaps you have deprived yourself of a good opportunity. It would be better to convert the warning signal into critical arguments, and to examine the man and the proposal. To check whether the actual values justify your preconception or whether they are in fact closer to your desired values: the right man, the best proposal. We would live in paradise if everyone did this. But we have no time, no patience, no desire, no comprehension—and put up with the mistakes. A costly convenience!

On the other hand, it really is absolutely impossible to receive and examine all existing information. If we refuse to do this with conscious processes, how much more must this apply to the sensorium of our body. It helps itself, with blocks and

A bite into a sour apple triggers the appropriate facial expression. Just the thought, the idea of what it will taste like, is enough to cause this mimicry.

through selection. A certain flow of information is blocked in order to let through more urgent information according to its priorities. Our senses make this choice almost automatically. If we are hungry, our eye is not caught by banks and shoe shops, but our glance lingers on every restaurant and cafe. An elegant woman will certainly not overlook a single boutique. The man at her side spots every bar.

This is an instance of selection by our control system, but not a dismissal of perceptions. The sense organs receive much more, but they do not burden our consciousness with everything. The subconscious simultaneously stores other information, too. Witnesses under hypnosis have given testimony of details of incidents which they could not remember in a conscious state, however hard they tried: car licence numbers, colour of clothing, etc.

We become aware of experiences through changes in our organism. The impulse for these changes can come from within our own body (hunger) or from outside, through stimuli. In both cases the body attempts to reestablish a balanced state, to get back into harmony. It satisfies the urge or reacts to the stimulus. Equilibrium is restored. Any disturbance of this harmonious balance means disorder, agitation. Then energy and vitality increase, and we display an unusual activity. In extreme cases the coordination of our movements breaks down, our voice cracks, our thoughts get confused. Conversely, when our energy decreases we can get into apathetic and depressive states, which can end up as complete indifference.

There is a direct and reciprocal interplay between urges and stimuli, our body vitality and our emotional state. We will now pursue this interaction.

Breathing supplies the body with the oxygen that is indispensable for the generation of energy. We can divide the process of breathing into three phases: inhaling, retention, exhaling. I like to compare it with the primary colours red, yellow, and blue, because in these transitions one passes through the whole range from warmth to cold, from positive to negative sensations.

Inhaling, the absorption of oxygen, provides us with strength, vitality, joy.

Exhaling causes the reduction of strength, loss of vitality, apathy, but also release of accumulated air.

Retention is the short period of time in which the body attempts to block all motion and the flow of information—an absolute standstill—in order to arrive calmly at a decision: concentration.

If we dive into ice-cold water we first hold our breath, then react precipitately. If alarmed, we quickly and sharply draw in our breath, in order to tank up on energy, and then hold our breath until we have decided on our reaction. Then we sharply let our breath out—like a karate expert when he strikes, or a discus thrower at the moment he releases the discus—in order to increase the power of our movement through this release action. But if our uncertainty continues, we falteringly breathe in more air, and this causes congestion and cramping up in our body, which can lead to response paralysis.

We are constantly breathing in and out; however, the rhythm and emphasis can change. In a harmonious state we breathe calmly, regularly, and with pleasure; our body relaxes when breathing out. If we're depressed, the emphasis is on slow exhalation, then a short standstill, and one breathes in only the absolute minimum amount of oxygen necessary. When agitated, we vacillate between extremes with varied emphasis in the breathing process. This mixed state reflects our mental condition, our mixed feelings. We are in a situation in which we do not want to accept one point, and cannot uphold the other, and therefore attempt to push away the entire conflict.

An extreme example explains this very clearly. A daughter comes home and admits that she is expecting a baby. It takes her father's breath away. He does not want to accept the fact, but he also cannot deny the information. He vacillates between wish and reality, and so his breath vacillates sharply between inhaling and exhaling. The rapid alternation accelerates the heartbeat and circulation, and the body again has to regulate this overactivity. It stops breathing, slows things down. The struggle between conflicting sensations is shifted to the body. Rapid breathing—retention, acceleration—slowing down.

Breathing and Rhythm

Tensions (left to right)

Hand on heart: This is an easy-going conversation with frank feelings.

Holding hands indicates a familiar and intimate atmosphere.

His left arm restricts her freedom and seems threatening. She draws back her hands and raises her knee in defence.

The threat is increased by his pointing forefinger. She shuts herself off with the movement of her right arm and leg.

The tension seems to have eased and the situation to be more relaxed. But in fact she is blocking him with her right elbow.

Here the blockade is maintained by her lowered arm.

Evidently something in the touch of her hand disturbs him: He protects himself with his raised knee.

She soothingly puts her hand on his knee to counter his aggressive posture, whereupon he lays back his head and exposes his throat with a provocative gesture against her hand movement, as if he were saying: You can't impress me with it, I'm not afraid of it.

48

Of course this is the description of a quasi-mechanical alternation process that takes place within the organism. But we experience this critical state of our body condition and are aware of it; the person with us recognizes it through the signals of our expression. It is our body's response to our brain and reflects the quality of relationship between us and the situation.

Here, too, we see that the rhythm of breathing and that of the heartbeat influence one another. Together they determine the rhythm of our movements. Conversely, our bodily activities like walking, running, sprinting, and so on affect the rhythm of our breathing and our heart. That is why we can recognize the emotional state of a person from the rhythm of his movements, and even influence it. If we want to soothe a child, we stroke her head with gentle, rhythmic movements. By dancing, rocking vigorously, or screaming, we can get our body into an excited condition, bring about a trancelike state. Through the rhythm of speaking and intonation, emotions and intentions can be signalled beyond the meaning of the word. A skillful actor can

If one does not want to accept some information or a perception, this is often indicated by blowing air out through one's mouth: I will not take this in!

put us into a state of great tension by properly using his voice, although he has only trivia to say; and a monotonous speaker can put us to sleep, even though he is talking about extremely exciting subjects.

Rhythm has been given us by nature; beating time has been invented by humans. Music is based on harmony and rhythm and animates us through the natural interaction with our body's rules of movement. A metronome beats perfect time. For us this rhythm is an expression of intention. We also sense and recognize this transition from spontaneous harmony to timed rhythm in movements: it announces the intervention of intent, is connected with a purpose.

A person wanders for hours through the woods. A clearing opens up and an inn comes into view. Want to bet that the hiker changes the rhythm of his steps, falls into a timed stride? He is heading for a goal.

Every person, we said, has his own rhythm, his individual walk. If someone—whether it is a politician or a political movement—wishes to make a group or a number of people toe the line toward the same goal, he sets a common pace, in step, in time. This works well, from military drills to demonstration marches. If one moves in the same timed rhythm as others, one easily feels in harmony with them.

We also give timed signals when we attract attention, demonstrate impatience, or conceal uncertainty. The departure from natural rhythm is noticeable. We have already grasped something and utter an accelerated yes-yes-yes, we tap our finger or some implement on the table or on our palm, tap our hand against our thigh, we adjust our body in timed movements—one, two, three—when we get ready to speak. All of these are timed impulses.

The pattern of movement reflects inner harmony or disharmony. Irregularity in rhythm and timing points to instability, a jerky movement to disturbance. From this we can learn that every feeling, every emotion is the consequence of a strong relationship between ourselves and a situation, an object, a wish. Without this relationship they do not affect us.

The difference between feeling and emotion is very great, but unfortunately most people do not make this distinction.

Feeling and Emotion

Feeling is everything that we receive through sensory perception. From outside we receive the feeling of cold or warmth, of form and structure of an object, sensations of smell or taste, and so forth. My equilibrium will not be disturbed by feelings; no conflict will arise. Because if I feel a desire, I fulfill it. If I am cold, I put on a coat; if I am warm, I take off my jacket; I avoid a bad taste; and I put my hands over my ears if I hear a loud noise. The same applies to internal feelings: tenderness and affection, pleasure and sickness. I express them in words and gestures, with flowers and attention, through communication and asking for participation. This is accepted and reciprocated, the personal relationship perceived in harmony.

Emotion is a disruption of one's equilibrium and results when something throws us off balance. If we do not fulfill our desires, cannot satisfy our feelings, they often take on the dimension of emotions. This can be very positive, like the sight of a beautiful landscape that overwhelms me, or the expectation

A movement full of feeling . . .

of a wonderful evening. More often, however, we register emotion as negative: Our loving affection is not reciprocated, we have given the wrong signals for our willingness, we are afraid of losing something or someone. Disappointment, uncertainty, and fear throw us off balance.

Emotion affects our whole body, and as long as its balance is disturbed, all our actions are affected. It is almost impossible to suppress emotions for any length of time; they will always become evident through signals, because every repression generates pressure and counterpressure, which seeks to find release to the outside. If we block these pressures, they turn to the inner organs, and reappear in psychosomatic disturbances: The body reacts to excess emotional pressure by getting sick. Just as excess pressure within a gas container is indicated by a dial, and releases itself through a valve, so emotionally caused excess pressure in the body is signalled through muscle tension or mimicry, and needs a valve. One can hold a fully inflated ball under water for some time, expending

. . . and an emotional movement.

much energy and concentration. But if one does this, energy is lacking somewhere else at the same time—I certainly cannot simultaneously concentrate on a conversation. That is why at some point we have to consciously allow our "ball," the emotional excess pressure, to come to the surface, or it will escape from our control and will pop up somewhere else.

An emotional person—in other words someone who does not always keep his feelings under the purposeful control of his head—is always positive: He openly shows us his position. His expression of emotions informs us of his relationship to a situation or position, and conveys his attitude and judgement. The expression of emotion is the most important communication signal between people. All contact is based on this subjective exchange of experience, since none of us can perceive objectively.

A mouth pursed for a kiss shows tenderness through a primeval signal, as if one wanted to feed a little bird.

Learning and Values

The perceptions of our feelings affect us pleasantly or unpleasantly. This sensation depends above all on the satisfaction that the stimulus arouses. We can connect enjoyment or pain, appetite or distaste, with the same intensity, and we adjust our judgement accordingly: good or bad. These values are transferred equally to associative secondary phenomena, from concrete to abstract experiences and expectations. The expectation of success makes us happy, the idea of failure "hurts our feelings." In the first case the body expresses its pleasure through relaxation, in the second case it responds with blocks and tension.

This relationship is used particularly intensively in advertising psychology, which works with promises of pleasure. This shows clearly how dependably the associative judgements of our body function, and to what extent the body can be manipulated by them. Take the cigarette advertisements. "Smoking satisfaction," a ride through the waving grasses of the prairie, the refreshing coolness of palms, beach and ocean waves, the feelings of freedom and nature—these are subjects used constantly—advertising signals. Our body is cradled in pleasant fantasies, we are "lulled" by the brand: It must be good. But how many people smoke with their feet stretched toward the campfire, a mustang whinnying in their ear, gazing at the Rocky Mountains? Actually, when we hear the word "cigarette," we should think of the stale smell of cafeterias and curtains, of smoke-filled bars and meeting halls, of harrowing conferences, long evenings, and the mornings after. But no. Our body, receiving the signals of nature, allows itself to be captivated by the association of wide expanses and freshness, and reacts with pleasant expectation. It suppresses the fact that this is not how they will be fulfilled, because nicotine, too, is a narcotic stimulant, something that one, of course, does not like to admit. (Who is going to advertise using this argument?!) Yet often enough our body signals us directly that the strong stimulus of this positive enjoyment also has negative consequences. But even when we learn that, we seldom act according to the unpleasant experience.

Learning results from repeating an experience, whereby we correct our encounter with this experience according to the feedback of the success or failure of our behaviour. As long as no value is established, the experimentation continues. The improvement and refinement of the appurtenant information saves energy, and the more accurate reaction brings us our desired goal more quickly.

If we have affixed the pragmatic value "good," we feel

compelled to repeat it; if the result is "bad," we will try to avoid such experiences. We have already pointed out the danger of precipitate definitions: Preconceptions provoke incorrect behaviour. We have stopped learning.

The longer we examine the experience—and that means learn—the more our chance, our possibility to develop grows. The learning process depends on our decision. As soon as I set a value, good or bad, sufficient or insufficient, I close the circle. The little grey cells are freed from their preoccupation with this experience, and turn to another task. But this does not have to be so. We could still go on learning. Instead of one foreign language—assessment: that's enough!—we could learn three or six. Instead of one pitiful piano piece—evaluation: that is bad, and too difficult!—we could have an elevating musical experience. Most of us have the technical abilities for it. It is up to us to decide: so far, and no further—to set a value. As a rule the body is capable of achieving more than we, through our voluntary decisions, give it credit for.

Promises of pleasure are one of the methods of advertising.

We constantly set priorities and thus declare that we do not have time for all those things. What is true about this is that with every new event or interest we change the order of precedence and time sequence of our experiences. One person wants to play the piano, the second wants to learn languages, and the third wants to lie in the sun. That's fine, to each his own decision. But the explanation "no time" for one thing or another is incorrect.

We always have time. How we organize it depends on our priorities; and whether we plan it correctly depends on whether we employ the appropriate priorities. We are usually under external or internal pressures that prevent us from carefully checking the actual value and desired value. In most cases the self-imposed desired value dominates. If an employee asks to talk to us about the problems of customer Jones while we are in the process of preparing for a meeting with the management about the expected returns of the coming quarter, then our "no" is probably setting the right priority. Not for sure, because maybe Jones is a major client, and we have just ignored this fact because of our blocked perception. But it is probable. If we are sitting at home in the evening, reading the paper, and our son timidly announces he is having a problem with his last bit of homework, then our "no" is probably setting a wrong priority. However, in both cases we claim: I do not have the time. What we really mean is: At this moment you are not on my priority list.

The desire for inner harmony, for a trouble-free, peaceful, and ordered life, tempts us to set our values very quickly. That saves time and conflicts, renewed examination and confrontation. This behaviour is not realistic, because the world is constantly changing and actually demands that we constantly change our values. The label good–bad is not enough.

When I returned from China people asked me what it was like. I did not understand. Well, was it good or bad? It was neither good nor bad: Okay, did it come up to your expectations? I said, "It was different." Were you disappointed? Maybe at first; then I corrected my course, and it was neither good nor bad: It was different.

China is everywhere. It is easier to judge, and thus block new experiences, than to compare the real actual values with the assumed desired values. Because with the judgements one not only jeopardizes bodily harmony, but often also compliance with social conventions. Learning is hard.

Description and Language

Higher animals like the primates, ape and man, developed a series of signals through living together in a group, signals that facilitate their communication. Imitation develops from observation, and a code of such means of communication develops from common experiences. To begin with, they are descriptions through gestures. A hand on the stomach and a face contorted with pain signals a stomachache. Here we are already combining various forms of expression into an abstract concept.

Activities are easily described through imitation: scratching, eating, walking, carrying, shovelling, etc. But through body posture, and above all through the graphic expressive powers of our mobile hands, we can also describe objects in such a way that others will understand.

But there are definite limits. The depiction of quite simple processes takes a great deal of time; when dealing with complicated ones, it is altogether questionable whether the other person grasps them accurately.

Natural sounds, an integral part of body language, are the first means of emphasis and the supplementation of such communication. Expressions of pain or joy, contentment or excitement, have definite forms in the sound pattern and sequence tones of the voice, and can be recognized. These sounds also transmit information over greater distances: signs of recognition, call, warning, and the like. Over thousands of generations man has developed a verbal language out of these primitive sounds.

The origins can still be found in the sound of our language and, in fact, in the language of all peoples. The phonetic sound of a word often sensually describes its substance: onomatopoeia. Water "gurgles" out of a bottle; in Hebrew the bottle itself is called "bak-buk." "Warm" is a pleasant feeling and a long drawn out melodious sound in contrast to the short "cold." In Italian almost the same tone sequence establishes the same association in reverse in "caldo" (hot) and the hard "fredo" (cold). In associative sounds like "slap" and "carressing" the nature and duration of the action can be sensed. If we listen carefully to our language, we can find this sensual quality of phonetic description in innumerable words.

Admittedly, through its abstractive capacity, verbal language has opened up a dimension to communication that reaches beyond the exchange of sensory experience practically without limit. Its content includes feelings and objects, conditions and processes, conceptions and associations. Whatever we feel or think, we can express—with some difficulty—in words and make intelligible to others. Because each person stores the same code in his brain as long as he continues to learn, and every new word he picks up has the same meaning in his "computer" as in the brains of millions of other people.

I say "table," and everyone knows: an inanimate object, a surface to eat at, write on, or put things on. But what kind of table? I say "a round glass table with a metal base," and everyone can imagine the table I am talking about. Perhaps they ask for certain details to make sure. If I say "a refectory table from the fifteenth century," I will have to explain it, describe it in detail for some people. But after that these seven words will mean to them that it is probably a very long, massive wooden table that used to stand in the refectories of monasteries. Surely this is fantastic: a whole world of imagery opens up because of a content of seven words!

We can note two things from this striking example. There is no concept and no abstraction without a concrete prototype. One has to be able to imagine a thing in order to have a concept of it. If this is the case, one can continue to develop ideas and concepts, move away from the concrete form by establishing values and meta-values; but if the person one is talking to no longer understands, one again has to revert to concrete experience and set up new lines of communication.

And secondly, this fantastic brain, as storage for information and instrument of communication, accomplishes more than any computer. There is no invention and no way of thinking that does not exist in the living organism. Even the computer is an invention of a brain and can only fulfill tasks set it by human thoughts. Its apparent superiority actually shows its limitations: It can work faster, combine information, and spit out data faster than our brain—but only because it is constructed and programmed for these special tasks. Considered from the point of view of the range of the computer's abilities, every brain is superior to it. And apart from that, the computer's information is always solely factual, it has no communicative quality or tonal shadings.

I consider information to be factual when it is delivered objectively on the level of technical description, of impersonal statement, when I state something without personal participation and opinion—and that is extremely rare. Because, in fact, something of my own opinion about this information is echoed in every sentence that I formulate, in every word I articulate. Every such opinion arouses in me and in others associative differences in vitality, which are also transferred to voice inflection and feelings. Every feeling, and particularly every emotion, mobilizes an energy exchange in the body, through which we experience this state. This, of course, also applies to the way we speak. If someone says: I am sad, I am content, I am happy, I am well—with an unchanging voice level and monotonous inflection, without the slightest emphasis of vitality—then, though the information is always clear, we would not accept it as such. It does not sound convincing because the relationship to the appropriate body condition and the state experienced is not perceptible. The verbal statement is obvious, but it is contradictory in the communicative context. The body negates what the word says through voice and posture. Speech and body have to be in harmony. The more strongly they impart the form of the experience together, the more convincing is the man and his statement.

This harmony also has to be established in reverse: when information comes from outside and is meant to replace an experience. What good is a pragmatic value that I accept, but that I have not examined for myself? Generally full-blown principles are the result, which are revealed to be lip service the moment they are burdened by personal experience. Let us take a painful example.

The mother is a widow, one aunt is divorced, the other unmarried, and a girl grows up with these three women in a small provincial town. They teach her that though one cannot entirely avoid men, they actually represent an extremely superfluous and particularly unreliable and annoying sample of the human race, which one should never get involved with. Since they have been convincing the girl of this all her life, this secondary experience becomes a firm concept for her. In school she talks in this vein and is considered to be crazy; she treats the boys accordingly, and is considered by them to be stuck-up. But then a boy comes along, and he is terrific. Now it is irrelevant whether she rejects him or gets involved with him—conflict is unavoidable. Her own knowledge of the feeling or the experience tell her that this is marvellous. The principles, the desired values in her head vehemently contradict it. And her mother and aunts are horrified. What should she trust now—the verbalized values, the critical comments of her relatives whom she considers to be authorities, or the persuasive powers of her own experience? Her entire personal value assessment is in question—what is good, and what is bad? She will now stumble through crises and have to reexamine everything that up till now had seemed familiar and natural—as if she had been reborn. This can be boiled down to the sentence: There are no experiences apart from those of one's own body. We are not truly ourselves until we are in harmony with it.

Is what we are familiar with natural, and what we are accustomed to normal? When we talk of natural behaviour, we imply harmony with nature, with biological legitimacy. But we do not mean it quite so literally. No human lives biologically correctly—even the life of the strictest environmentalist is full of compromises—and if we all wanted to go back to nature with Rousseau, then in our overpopulated regions we would neither have enough caves to shelter in nor enough trees to climb. We cannot retreat from the point already reached in the development of civilization, and can survive only through sensible application of human progress. It is an old nostalgia and a beautiful dream—but in practice the phenomenon "nature" and the concept "natural" can no longer be reconciled with human behaviour toward nature. We call our behaviour "natural" when we are used to behaving a certain way, and claim that it is normal. Deviations from this norm appear to us to be strange, arbitrary, and unnatural. This applies to us as well as to others. If I am used to reacting calmly, I will consider a state of agitation with uncontrolled reactions to be unnatural. Even if I connect expansive gestures and flamboyant behaviour with the image of another person as a matter of course, I will still consider such behaviour in myself, or in a third person who uses quiet gestures, to be improper and will not accept it. The violation of habit and expectation confuses me, causes a breach in the relationship and is declared "unnatural." And in this sense, but only in this sense, everyone follows his own nature. It is the mark and trait of his character and individuality.

The judgement whether the movement is natural or "normal" presumes observation and knowledge of the customary mode of expression of this person. In some cases the reasons for this deviation from usual behaviour are immediately obvious, and therefore we accept it, or gain further knowledge about that person. He is under strong emotional pressure, like deep sorrow or effusive joy, and so he behaves in a completely unfamiliar way. Accepted, then: A new behavioural pattern is discovered and registered. He finds himself in an unexpectedly embarrassing situation or a personal dilemma and proves to be surprisingly tense and awkward. Accepted: We have gained new insight. And such behavioural experiences also apply to us. Through observing ourselves, we learn what changes our behaviour is subjected to in particular situations—find it to be artificial, arbitrary, unnatural ourselves. But it is merely an unmastered variation of our own natural behaviour.

The naturalness of a person is the expression of his individuality. We identify every figure and every individual

Individuality and Normality

60

according to categories of form and colour, of smell and sound, of type and intensity of movement and so on. The combination and the emphases of these categories are registered as typical characteristics of this individual: traits of his identity. Every human being has received his elementary characteristics through genetic information: physiognomy and stature, temperament and vigor. They distinguish him from all other humans, and he cannot lose them. No one can lose himself, therefore he also cannot ''find'' himself. One can only find something one has lost; our problem is rather to accept ourselves as we are. A person can lose his orientation and goal, and question his own life, the purpose of life. But he can neither lose nor question himself, his identity. Nevertheless, he can change, since the greater part of our individual characteristics are acquired, not innate.

Luckily one cannot change acquired behaviour overnight, since the effect would be pretty devastating for us. Someone who behaves completely differently from one day to

Even expansive gestures can seem natural.

the next seems unnatural, artificial, strange. One should stay in harmony with one's natural behaviour, but one also has to be aware of the fact that the information that one transmits through one's body and its forms of expression decides what effect he or she has on others. If I come to the conclusion that my effect on others does not correspond with my intentions or conceptions, I try to correct it, verbally or through the language of my body. But this must not happen too suddenly, since we assess people according to whether their behaviour fits or does not fit our accustomed expectations. If certain images and forms do not meet with these expectations, are not controlled, and seem put on, this behaviour is felt to be unfitting and immediately the whole person seems untrustworthy. We have no confidence in him, and everything goes wrong for him.

On the whole we change our behaviour gradually through the insights that we accept, through convictions and views we adopt, or through people with whom we live or whom we admire. Their behaviour rubs off on us; as one says, they are our prototype. At first even this change seems strange to others whom we meet less frequently, and it demands of them a new attitude because the actual value no longer corresponds with their desired value. Naturally this is irritating, disturbing, and easily leads to the annoyed complaint: But you were always like that before!—as if one always had to stay the same. However, people do change, because of strokes of fate or war experiences, because of career changes or imprisonment—we all know of examples which can alter one's physiognomy and one's whole behaviour. Actually they change constantly with age and everyday experiences. It is up to us continually to be prepared for this, to accept it, to correct our image and to set up new ways of communication.

It is important that we critically include ourselves in this process of constant change. Someone surprises us with a totally unfamiliar gesture and we point this new habit out to him. He will vehemently deny this fact, or at least its novelty, because as far as he is concerned, it became a habit long ago, and he is no longer really aware of it. The same applies to us. It is like someone who lives next to a busy railway line. He no longer notices the regular recurring noise, but at least subconsciously he will register if the 4:20 train is cancelled and there is a deviation from the natural repetition.

So we, too, have to ask ourselves: Am I aware of the fact that I constantly send out signals that affect others? If I ignore or deny this, I am constructing a hermetically sealed world for myself, a subjective view of the world, and I remove myself from the game. What I really should ask is: Who is sending the stimulus in the interrelationship between me and my environment, and who is responding with a reflex? Is what I am receiving feedback—the response to a stimulus emitted by me—or am I really the first to react to a stimulus, does the feedback begin with me?

No individual is free of values and valuations. What I experience is not always what the other person really wants to tell me, it is often a response to my own unconscious behaviour. He is aggressive toward me, but perhaps he is not the aggressive instigator; rather, have I emitted stimuli that make him react that way? Actually he came to me with a friendly request, but I was lost in thought, and glanced out of the window, was abstracted and aloof, or played with the car keys that he had placed on the table in front of him. Thus the request turned into a demand. It takes two to communicate, and the communication arises out of stimulus and response. Relatively often, the way we behave forces the other person into a role he had not intended. We create a situation, and he has no choice but to respond to our stimuli and play by our rules.

When I am apprehensive without direct cause or identifiable reason, my senses are highly sensitized. They now function as an alarm system and interpret every movement and every person coming close to me as a danger. If someone comes up to me, stretches out his hand, or simply stands there waiting, I register this as a threat. However friendly his intentions are, my fear is stronger and brands him as an aggressor. I force him into this role, and I continue to be suspicious even when he steps back from this close range that I consider to be threatening.

If a woman is extremely distrustful of men, she will interpret negatively every sign of a man's advances or affection and will try to find the evil intentions behind them: He wants to trick me, get me into bed, make me dependent, whatever. She builds up an attitude to relationships that eliminates almost any chance of open communication right from the outset.

What role does body language play in this interaction? There is an inseparable connection between muscle movements and inner feelings. An experiment clearly illustrates this: Raise your eyebrows—and now be aggressive. It is not really possible, you look rather funny. But draw your eyebrows together, and you succeed in looking aggressive. A body movement can block feelings. It can also generate them. And it affects another person as a stimulus, even before we realize it.

Muscle movements also determine our feelings: You cannot look aggressive if you raise your eyebrows.

We have acquired the greater part of the mimicry, movements, and gestures with which we express ourselves to others through imitation or upbringing. They serve to describe our feelings, and despite all our subjectivity and individuality, they are a universally binding code. Conversely, this also means that the way of moving we have acquired also influences our feelings.

Upbringing is the attempt to plan the reaction of people, so that we can plan with this group of people. It works best in the narrow circle of the family, in which everyone learns his manner of expression and movement. The next stage of this common code is represented by the social stratum to which the

Conditioned Reflexes

family belongs. Then there are norms of behaviour set by peer groups—those people with whom one has direct social intercourse—and the conditions of the working world and one's occupation. We have already mentioned that not only individual characteristics but also a person's social position and social status can be recognized from the traits of his body language. This finally extends as far as the so-called typical characteristics of nationality or particular cultural groups—a typical Englishman, Italian, or Swede, a South European, or an Oriental.

How do these "typical" features originate? How can one say that there is a plan in upbringing that purposefully transfers social standards and the respective order of this society to the next generation? Pavlov's *Investigation of Conditioned Reflexes* shows us how easily this happens. Pavlov discovered that apart from innate, natural reflexes of an organism, there is also a system of learned reactions, similar to the reflex system, and he called it "conditioned" reflexes.

The experiment that Pavlov used to prove his hypothesis is as simple as it is convincing. Whenever a dog got something to eat, a red light was turned on. There were two simultaneous signals: eating and light. The gastric juices start to function, food is waiting. By repeating this experience, the two signals, eating and light, are connected. One day the light goes on, but there is no food there. The dog sees that his bowl is empty, but his body reacts as if the food were there—the gastric juices are stimulated, the expectation of food determines his reaction. The red light triggers this expectation: a reflex action, a conditioned reflex. Admittedly it is illogical to react that way, since the proof to the contrary is given through sensory perception. Eyes, nose, tongue say: no food. Yet the body still reacts.

This method is also employed in upbringing. Certain needs and experiences are connected to secondary phenomena, and eventually the person reacts not only to the primary signal, but to the secondary one. For instance when we are eating, a certain kind of good conduct is coerced first by refusal, then rewarded with increased giving. Therefore the form of this giving promises the satisfaction of needs, and can be attained through the good conduct. At some point the form of giving itself triggers the good conduct, which is disconnected from the reason "food"—a conditioned reflex. This is not bad in itself. But it does mean that through repeating experiences and observations and their association with secondary phenomena—like reward and punishment—we can train our behaviour, and manipulate any number of reactions. These conditioned reflexes are not programmed into the innate genetic code, they are instilled by means of repeated association of experiences. Usually they then function as reliably as natural reflexes.

I would like to mention a few very explicit examples of the effect of such social standardization. A man has every reason in the world to respond to a serious insult by punching the other person—natural reflex. But the other person is a woman; then there is a threshold of restraint, a conditioned reflex. In a local bar a group of men are noisily telling each other obscene jokes, and a priest enters the room—embarrassed silence, conditioned reflex. Or an example of the conscious use of conditioned reflexes: Of what use is all the discipline and mechanical drill in armies and on parade grounds, if it is not to teach people to react against their natural escape reflexes through the conditioned reflexes of automatic action in a case of war, whether they are marching into the line of fire, or handling their weapons with deliberate movements.

Upbringing is the basic introduction into social behaviour. It has its own methods in the family, then in the social group, the cultural group, the nation, the cultural area. In this way the circle of people to whom the same identification forms apply expands concentrically. This possibility of common identification is indispensable, because a group can only exist if the reactions of all its members are predictable. Group life cannot develop without order and planning. Elementary order is given by nature and by our genetic code. A society now has to see to it that all its members will have the same responses to specific stimuli. If one knows that people will react in a specific way in one instance, and in a different way in another, one can make plans with them and for them, plans that they will probably follow.

Planning improves the odds of desired behaviour. In order to increase the probability of success, one has to decrease the risk of deviation. The simplest solution is to block uncontrolled spontaneity and emotions. To do this one only needs to master behavioural expression and have it under control. In order to stimulate the desired behaviour, one uses reward and punishment. Praise, love, and public recognition accompany behaviour that serves the good of the society—the Plan. Withdrawal of love, contempt, and graduated punishment are threatened and carried out when a certain kind of behaviour interferes with the common aims of the group or society. The Plan also includes developing each subtle means of conditioning

66

as individual bad conscience or collective guilt feelings. The more developed and complex the forms of a society, the greater is the compulsion to plan. It is easy to see that highly industrialized countries—just like nations with a rigidly centralized or dictatorial structure of administration!—have the strictest systems of upbringing. It is the degree to which organization is necessary that retroacts on the rigorousness of the forms of upbringing. On the other hand, one can see that Mediterranean countries with less industrialization, or with a more agricultural character, have a more relaxed manner of upbringing, and offer more room for improvisation.

We can verify what has been stated here in general terms, through our own experience. From our birth we hear: A good child is one who obeys his parents' wishes, and praise and love are the reward. A child who follows his own desires is a bad child, and the punishment is anger and withdrawal of love. A good man and upright citizen is one who obeys the central political plan without protest; one who practices opposition and

Totally involuntary—but how quickly upbringing becomes like animal training.

demands changes is suspected of being a bad citizen. A man who makes use of what latitude he can, a nimble mind, is very quickly perceived as a restless spirit, or even a troublemaker. He who discreetly stays on the right track will in the end receive the distinguished service medal for civil behaviour. Is it surprising that our whole upbringing aims at a meager repertoire of movement?

The simpler the vocabulary of movements, the better suited it is for manipulation; the richer the vocabulary of movement, the more difficult it is to control. In language we develop the supplement to body expression that is necessary for social communication. Since language enables us to communicate in a very simple and unambiguous way, it is of principal interest in our upbringing, and our body vocabulary remains poor. (Language also offers a second advantage: Verbal language is an arranged code, and in its substance already a vehicle of the plan. The body reacts spontaneously, but language is subjected to the norm and is itself an instrument of control.)

Self-Assurance

Upbringing is carried out in two ways: through gesticular and verbal instructions on one hand, and on the other through the stimulus to imitate the behaviour of others. Through imitation, children adopt certain movement patterns of their family, young people and adults take on certain manners of their environment. In this way the human being adapts to the wealth or poverty of the possibilities for emotional experiences in his immediate environment. He accepts their characteristics or resists them, maintains his individuality. Two examples of this come to mind.

Imagine a family whose characteristic it is to walk around with sunken, caved-in chests, the expression on their faces hardly changing. It is certain that in this family not much is directly and spontaneously experienced or discussed. Emotions are suppressed, so that no stimuli will be generated, and no confrontation will arise, and all family members feel quite at ease, because they all move in the same way. One cannot talk about right or wrong, about a positive or negative way of behaving. Because for this group it is positive in their way.

But in this same family there can be a child who moves completely freely, according to his own rhythm. One can envy or admire him for this independence, or one can hate him

68

because it disrupts the structure. One thing is certain: There cannot be a balanced relationship, free of conflict, between the child and the others. The child confronts the others with expansive movements, expansive emotions, expansive experiences, none of which they are used to. He forces them to take a position and assimilate experiences that they want to avoid. They will feel more at ease when the child is not around, but at the same time miss him even with his provocation—a legitimate ambivalence of feelings.

But where did this child get its entirely different behavioural pattern, since he is growing up in the same environment? Well, it can be easier to bring up and train a particular child than it is another, but above all, the basic rhythm of every child is individual. Just as we come in all shapes and sizes, so for each of us the selective assimilation of our environment varies individually. Two children in the same family can develop very differently, because each one assimilates according to his own evaluation. One child will deny himself an intense experience (and the repetition of this pleasant encounter) because he is afraid of his father's reproachful look and desperately needs reward and recognition. He wants to be a good child. The other child values this encounter and the experience connected with it more than he fears punishment. That child's evaluation is different, and he is prepared to bear the consequences of his family's opposition for the sake of this more intense experience. In this way the child asserts his original rhythm over the attempt to make him conform to the others.

The same thing that determines the pressure to adapt in this family applies to the pattern of upbringing in the planned society. One tries to get the people to experience less, to be content with a smaller vocabulary, to react functionally, to suppress their emotions, not to probe into individual possibilities. Rational thinking and functional actions are seen as positive basic values. Emotionalism is suspect, is considered to be a weakness, and inspires fear. But can we live without emotions? Far from it! Emotions form our strongest motivations and our clearest means of communication. If someone tells me about his emotions, or expresses them, I can understand him better, and he feels I accept him as he is.

For example, a meeting slowly drags on, bringing no results, and leaving everyone frustrated. Suddenly one of the employees bursts out with a spontaneous comment, and a surprisingly simple suggestion. What happens? He is promptly reprimanded by the startled gathering: You are being highly emotional! Not one of them considered whether there was

Even when a child turns a cold shoulder and demonstrates protest, patient explanation on his level will prompt him to open up his attitude.

anything to his suggestion: It was simply emotional, and therefore inappropriate. Result: An opportunity is wasted, and an employee antagonized. If the boss then sends him away with some work, he will be faced with a pile of insoluble problems. He feels overworked, tired, goes home at five, and plays tennis for three hours.

How differently this situation could have developed if his reaction had been accepted. What motivation could there have been for him and other employees, if one had considered his suggestion, had discussed it, and then said: I understand you, you are looking for a solution, like the rest of us, let's try it this way. It would have motivated the employee—who himself knows that a spontaneous idea first has to be thoroughly examined, and that then a decision has to be made with one's head—and it would also have given the others courage to recall all options at their disposal, and to implement them.

Emotion is only a weakness if we do not recognize it as such. If we are aware of our emotions—admit that they are

Self-assurance: I contentedly lean back from my writing desk. I have reached my decision, established my position, and now I am prepared to defend it with my elbows against any assault.

exam fever, or a weakness toward women, or dread of difficult decisions, or overconfidence—and they are accepted as such by others, they can become a stimulant for and instrument of better communication. Then we are not afraid to tell someone: I like you very much, but I have to say no to your suggestion because there's nothing in it for me. And the other person will not be offended, but will understand that on a different occasion we may well be able to get together. But if we, suppressing our emotions, instantly and formally say no, and close the door with relief, will the other person come again?

We not only have to live with our emotions, we should also show them, and learn how to deal openly with them. We can yield to them; then the consequence is lack of self-control. We can suppress them; then in the end they explode with uncontrolled force. Both things happen often enough. But if we are conscious of ourselves, are aware of our own emotions, accept those of others and acknowledge them to one another, we will find better equilibrium and harmony. We react emotionally with our heart, we make decisions with our head. And how often our head says no when our heart desires something. Too often, it seems to me, because we do not trust the persuasive powers of our emotions, and too seldom have the kind of self-assurance that allows our head to deal with them.

Walking Upright

Man is the creature that walks upright. When, at some time during the chain of evolution, a primate stood up on its hind legs, got accustomed to using them as its sole tools of locomotion and its front limbs as manipulatory instruments, the history of man began. In infancy every human being reenacts this millennia-long evolution within a few months. It is natural for the infant to move on all fours as soon as his muscles are strong enough. There are hardly any problems of balance. But all around the child, everyone else is moving on two legs. The urge to imitate compels the child to try this, too. He uses a bed, the leg of a chair, the corner of a table to help him get up. But it is difficult to get the body in balance in this stretched position. The baby collapses in a heap. He repeats the exercise, falls. He repeats it, staggers, falls. He keeps on repeating this until he is standing, then standing without help. It is a wonderful process, and it is not surprising that all parents feel it as a profound experience.

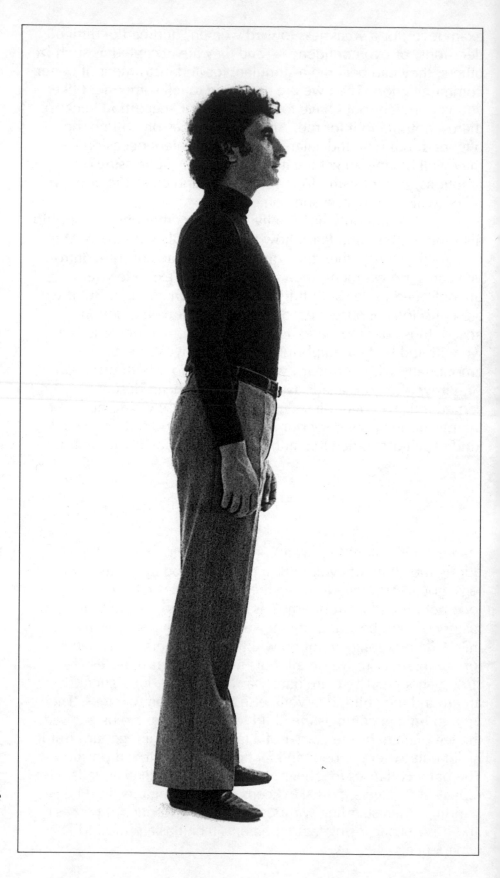

Muscle tone: We can literally feel the energy streaming up to the head through all our limbs, and filling our body with tension.

It is rather complicated to stand erect, to control all one's joints in order to utilize the vertical extension of the body. Of course we, like all animals, have muscles to do this. But in other animals the energy flow that fills these muscles with tension goes from the front to the back; you only need to watch how a four-legged animal gets up from a lying position and starts to move. Only in man has this flow developed a new direction because of the upright walk: It goes from the bottom to the top. But one still has to learn to mobilize this energy flow from the feet to the head, to attain the necessary muscle tone. Muscle tone is the tension that the muscles need to hold the body erect. When utilizing it correctly, man stands erect and steady in a relaxed posture. And this in itself is a miracle. One just has to compare the narrow sole of the foot and the slimness of the ankle with the length of the body!

Then comes the next—no, the first—step. Hands and arms are free and can become active. They are used—awkwardly at first, later as a matter of course and unconsciously—to help our balance in order to set our body in motion. A new danger: All our joints have only just been put in the position of carrying our body erect through the correct energy and muscle tone. Now, with a new energy flow and muscle tone they also have to set our upright body in motion, to make it move forward! Can it be done? Too much energy, too little equilibrium: The baby topples over. He picks himself up—that much he can do!—and tries again to walk. Imitation and repetition are the stimuli and means eventually to learn the impossible, something that has not been granted, and cannot be taught, to any other animal: walking upright.

We take earthly wonders so much in stride that we do not even notice the simplest of them, forget about their diversity. Because it is not enough that the human being alone is distinguished from the billions and billions of all creatures on this earth through his upright walk. Each of the billions of humans on this earth has his own way of walking, standing, moving, and expressing. And this posture and motor pattern is an open book of his habits and inclinations; of values that he has consciously set himself, and those that guide him unconsciously. But, of course, first one has to learn to read the signs and signals of body language.

Signs and Signals

Posture

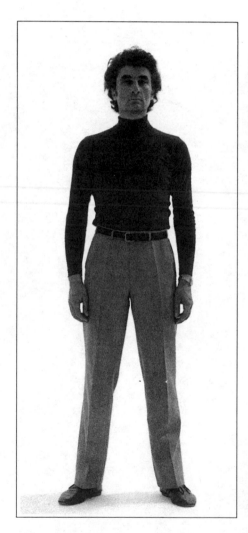

Objectively we are standing up straight when our body is in equilibrium without muscular effort. Our head rests horizontally on our neck, and our eyes are looking straight ahead. Our shoulders are squared, our hands and arms hang loosely, parallel to our body. Head, neck, and spine are brought into a straight line, our rib cage hangs on the vertebral column without pressing or pulling. Our squared pelvis supports the parts of the body resting on it; our legs, placed the width of the pelvis apart, create the direct connection with the ground, carry the total weight of our body, which is equally divided between the heel and the ball of the foot. We have brought our whole skeletal frame into a vertical line and our body becomes stabilized through the force of gravity; it is as if it were being held by a string from above. The energy flows steadily through our muscles up and down our body, and creates a flexible connection to the ground and space. As long as this is happening, we are in harmony with the world.

Any resistance and any disturbance of this posture either dams up this flow of energy or drains it. This can be demonstrated quite simply.

Objectively, very few people really stand up straight. What they subjectively consider to be a straight posture is in most cases a forward-leaning one that burdens the spine with some muscular strain. If this position is corrected to an objectively straight posture, and the upper body is pulled back, most people have the feeling they will fall backward, or conversely, land on their face.

This is another example of the fact that everyone registers what he is accustomed to as being correct: A man will claim that he is objectively standing straight, although it is not true and he merely subjectively feels it. Objectively, this person is constantly and considerably burdening his body energy because every deviation from the objectively straight posture demands considerable expenditure of energy. In order to establish equilibrium and hold the body upright, we have to compensate for these differences in load. For instance if the rib cage is pulling backward, the stomach is automatically pushed forward.

One can read variations of body expression and human individuality from the way someone stands straight. A person who stands with the soles of both his feet in good contact with the ground and imparts the feeling of stability by his posture is generally a realistic person. He knows where he stands, "he stands with both feet firmly planted on the ground." If, on the other hand, his toes dig into the ground—something, admittedly, that because of shoes one can usually only conclude from a change in the muscle tone—then it is a sign of insecurity, as if he felt the ground could slip away from under his feet. Such people will also cling to their opinions and attitudes.

Actually this is a very obvious association, and it's rather surprising that one has to explain it. As long as someone stands on one point, he wants to be sure of this point, and not be dislodged from it: it is his standpoint. If I want someone to change his stance and attitudes, be receptive to my arguments, I must also try to get him physically away from his standpoint: He has to change his position. Only a body movement away from this point stimulates new impulses in the body, and thus new ideas and considerations. If I myself notice that I am repeating my arguments, I also have to change my position. This brings a different frame of mind, new blood, and new stimulations—a new flow of thoughts and ideas, and other arguments.

When people dictate letters and memos, when they try to come up with new conceptions or creative new ideas, they often get up from time to time, walk to and fro, and apparently move around aimlessly and pointlessly. What they are actually doing is stimulating their body and brain, receiving varied impulses. They "pace off" their standpoints. Whether this happens consciously or unconsciously, in this way one bypasses the danger of getting stuck on one point, of getting caught up.

One must also seek to induce a similar effect in meetings and negotiations, if the situation becomes difficult and standpoints harden. A diverting question, the offer of a drink, an admiring comment about a picture on the wall is often enough to cause a change in movements and stimulations. Spontaneous interruptions or consciously planned breaks serve the same purpose: to approach a topic from a new angle. The movement changes the situation. Of course there are stubborn people who move where they want, and the way they're supposed to, and still remain stiff-necked and rigid, even when repeating their arguments and requests. They are stuck. In fact, they are then avoiding any movement that goes too far away from their standpoint, as one can see on videotapes of such conversational exercises. If one watches their physical behaviour

Standpoints

Stereotypes of body posture

*Standing with the knee of the free leg
bent towards the other looks
"effeminate"; standing with legs apart
"masculine."*

from beginning to end, one can see that their body position
hardly changed. They stuck to the official line and delivered
their prepared information, but that is as far as it went, no
conciliation of standpoints. There is a much-discussed political
formulation in East-West relations that illustrates the danger and
hope of such small changes in movement at the highest level:
change through conciliation. If one wishes to draw closer, one
has to change one's standpoints.

And now a further demonstration, which falls into the

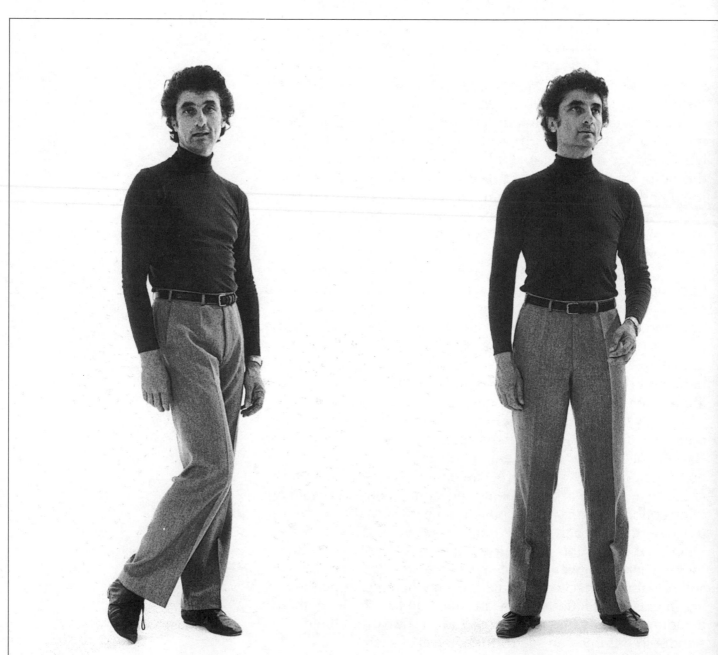

category of all stereotyped crime-series. If one wishes to intimidate and immobilize someone, one has to pin him down to his standpoint. The suspect sits on a chair, if possible mesmerized by harsh light, and the commissioner immobilizes him from behind, from the side, often from an unexpected position, with his questions, systematically encircles him, takes away any chance of escape, nails him to the point: Where were you at such and such a time, what were you doing? And finally the standpoint is clear—he takes the stand and confesses.

A sunken chest is a sign of inactivity.

A head-oriented person. The head thrust forward asserts: I can explain everything better! Chest and hands are held back and signal: Let someone else do it!

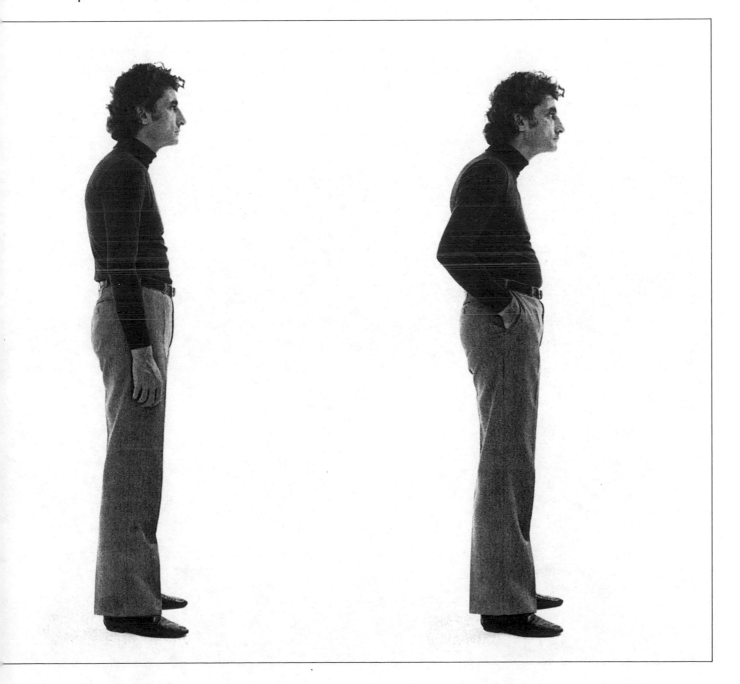

The man who does not take risks: small, cautious steps; neck and shoulders are locked, hands are inactive (see p. 89).

The man with curbed ambition: long strides, their vigor curbed by the raised toes (see p. 91).

Incidentally, it should be noted here that the dogged position of the boss behind his desk, or the fixed seating order around a conference table, with its standard positions, follows similar aspects of dominance. Freedom of movement is limited, responsibility—not response—expected.

If the energy flows upward, away from our feet, we are in danger of also losing the firm foundations of reality, and becoming disoriented. Contact with our roots is disturbed. We often say of people as well as arguments: They haven't got a leg to stand on.

To compensate for this process, the upward-flowing energy relatively often accumulates in the chest and head, and turns to the world of wishes, fantasy, future expectations, and planning. Thus respiration also means inspiration.

If the energy accumulates in a person's chest area, so

that he constantly walks around with puffed-up chest, so-to-speak, it is actually a sign of fear, which of course becomes noticeable in other ways. A person who does not give up this energy in his thoracic cavity is "holding back." He sticks to rules and agreements, is compelled to achieve, and is proud of it. The breath held back in his chest shows the willingness to act. This person is just as ready to carry out his superior's wishes as to acquire power himself.

A sunken chest, with shoulders rounded and bowed forward, conveys, not by chance, the impression of a great burden. These people are weighed down by worries that they are not equal to the demands made on them.

If the chest is pulling backward, the first thing one recognizes is the attempt to correct, to increase the distance to another person. Secondly, this rigid backward inclination of the

The man under pressure: The energy accumulates in the thoracic cavity, bursting to be released—but strictly according to rules and conventions.

The man under self-imposed blockade: Head and neck are held back, the shoulders tense, and his whole body is propelled forward only by the movement of his feet (see p. 85).

chest can also be recognized as an attempt to hold back feelings, to reduce physical activity to a minimum. Such people are inclined to cling firmly to preconceived opinions.

A person who draws back his shoulders and upper body is withdrawing. He is alarmed by a subject, or someone gets too close to him; maybe he is also afraid of his own courage to pursue a desire that could lead to a confrontation. To be on the safe side, he indicates in advance that he is ready to keep clear.

If the energy accumulates in the knees, they are straightened, the joints are locked. This signal means: I will not let myself be moved from my spot—and this stubborn determination also applies to intellectual and emotional reactions.

When the head is drawn in, the neck shortened, this also points to inflexibility and rigid adherence to a position. Such a person does not avoid a confrontation, because then he would have to move the perpendicular line of head and neck away from the center line.

If the head is held back, it blocks the neck and thus mobility: reserved attitude, very aloof. It takes tremendous effort to get close to such a person.

In contrast, if someone thrusts his head forward, it is as if he were on the lookout for initial information, so as to follow with his whole body later. If he is a curious person, one also notices the flexible neck and darting glances: He never sticks to one point for long, because he could then miss something somewhere else. One often sees this attitude in demonstrably intellectual people. It is as if they were sending the best part of themselves, their head, ahead into the battle. The rest of their body remains relatively expressionlessly behind the line, because it could easily express itself through feelings that are considered irritating and disturbing for this kind of observation.

The pelvis takes on a key position in the middle of the body. It connects the legs to the upper part of the body and thus it is at the mercy of the effects of all energy compensation. In a sense, emotions, feelings, and urges have their origin in the pelvis—this is obvious from the anatomy and physiology of the body. This, too, is the reason why the pelvic region is the great taboo zone of our body. A supple pelvis indicates an open attitude to one's own feelings and emotions: This person will not let himself be forced into the straitjacket of social taboos.

If someone stands with his pelvis rigidly drawn in at the front, and also with a sunken chest, we should interpret it as an extremely passive attitude. It expresses: Here I am, do what you

A man who respects social taboos: His withdrawn pelvis impedes any impulsive reaction.

want, but leave me in peace, and do not force me into any activity.

A pelvis that is withdrawn or pulled to the back indicates considerable reserve and regard for all social taboos. Even if the pelvis seems to be loaded with energy, no impulsive reactions can be expected. These are people who are very dependent on the opinion of others, stick to conventions, and insist on concepts like loyalty, family, and morality.

The Two Halves of the Body

We must divide the body into a left and a right side. The right side of the body is controlled by the left side of the brain. This is both the seat of the intellect, rational actions, and logical thinking, and the centre of speech. Marked preference to put all one's weight on one's right foot, actually markedly active right parts of the body in general, suggest that rational thinking and logical actions claim dominance over the emotions. A specially active right hand reveals the desire for action.

The left side of the body is controlled by the right half of the brain, to which one attributes emotional expression. People who show marked preference to stand on their left foot are more likely to act intuitively and let their feelings sway them. Sentimentality and artistic talents are no strangers to them. Naturally one can also draw the reverse conclusions: A passive left half of the body indicates passiveness of emotional qualities, a passiveness of the right half of the body points to passiveness of rational characteristics.

In reality, of course, people waiver or vacillate between feelings and reason, and we will seldom meet anyone in whom the dominance of one side of the body is all that clearly pronounced.

For instance, oversensitive people whose feelings have been hurt may run away from their feelings and prefer to stand on their right foot, with their left only in very cautious contact with the ground. Therefore everything always depends on the situation and our observations. The more we sharpen our attention to such left-right shifts, the more insight we gain into the attitude of a person in a specific situation, into the change of emphasis or priorities. Someone may shift his weight from his left leg to his right in the middle of a sentence: He has probably now changed over from feeling to logic. This could be true, but

Free leg, standing leg, right and left: The man has said goodbye, and is now seeking a firm foothold on his right leg, so as not to yield to his feelings any longer.

maybe his foot was hurting, or he remembered something totally different, which has nothing to do with this situation. Therefore one must assess such shifts very carefully and not overrate them. However, if I notice that the person I am talking to is constantly disposed toward the left, I can draw the conclusion that he is seeking emotional contact and would like to be accepted. In this case it is certainly more than a coincidental impulse, and I can verify this verbally or through my behaviour in the specific situation.

Ways of Walking

Walking is a conscious purposeful movement: Either we are moving toward a destination or we are running from a confrontation. In the latter case the more or less conscious place of refuge is the destination. At the same time walking is a very difficult balancing act. Every step means that we are leaving a safe foothold to reach another. Since we have a large number of joints, our organism has to make a very precise calculation of energy and statics when the body is propelled from the firm foothold in a specific direction, whereby it balances on one leg for a short while and then the entire shifted weight has to be caught by the other leg. This is, after all, not merely a movement forward, sideways, or backward; the body must simultaneously be held upright. Every step is a danger of which we are, of course, no longer conscious, because we have become accustomed to it. And in addition to all this, everyone has his own individual way of walking, and every emotion, every feeling, and stimulus instantly colours his way of walking and marks its nuances. It is not by chance that in all European languages we find the same word for the state of bodily and spiritual equilibrium: "Balance"—the connection is that direct and obvious.

One's way of walking is also subject to other changes. Intention of and reason for the movement, condition of the body, and age play an important role. In order to explain the whole complex of movements and what it states, one must analyse the individual components, because each manner of walking is made up of innumerable variations of the interaction of all body parts and their forms of expression, and thus naturally also reflects the conflicts or state of harmony of the organism at that time.

When one walks in a balanced smooth way, the upright line of the body between head and pelvis is maintained. The whole length of the leg is propelled forward from the knee. The pelvis retains its centre of gravity while the knee moves forward between hip and ankle joints. As the leg is stretched, the foot is placed on the ground, and it is not until this moment that the body transfers its total weight from the other leg to the foot that has now reached safe ground. Since the weight has been removed, the other leg can now execute the next step in the same way. The hands move loosely next to the body, assist its balance, and emphasize the motion of the specific walking rhythm. The eyes look straight ahead, head and neck are exposed in the vertical line, and through their flexibility make it possible to take in information all around with eyes and ears. This walk appears confident and open, is neither propelled

forward by ambition nor held back by fear. But now we will
look at deviations from this steady walk.

A head that is thrust back automatically blocks the flexibility of the neck (see p. 79). Thus the walk also becomes rigid and stiff, follows a straight line, and does not admit any information from either side, for it could only distract from the planned destination. It is the walk of people who have a firmly established view of the world, who keep exactly to their guidelines. This way of holding the head is often combined with a rigid attitude of the chest in which energy accumulates, and this surely indicates that the person attaches great importance to conventions and is dependent on social recognition.

I call this type the "blinkered man" and like to tell the story of the smart farmer who had a willful horse. It was constantly being distracted by tufts of grass on the edge of the field to the left, and the oats to the right. So the clever farmer put blinkers on the horse, so it could only look straight ahead. From then on the horse ploughed straight furrows, just as the farmer wanted. The "blinkered man" is just as dependable. He is indispensable in every party, in the bureaucracy, the finance department, and every position where imagination merely gets in the way, and accurate execution is of prime importance.

In contrast to this, people whose head and neck are in constant lively motion while they are walking are people who take an interest in absolutely everything and are continually collecting information. Naturally they are also distracted by it, but this is balanced out by the extensive acquisition of information. These people always have ideas and suggestions ready, they can be employed especially in conceptual planning and in public offices, wherever one has to keep up to date. Of course, whether they also finish everything that they start and suggest depends on whether their ability to put things into practice is well enough developed and functions quickly enough.

If the head is thrust forward, it slightly impairs the movement of the neck, the field of vision, and quick reactions. These people are cautious. They send their eyes ahead, keep a lookout, and can then withdraw their head in time, as if they had never been there, had never seen anything. We have already mentioned the intellectual variety of the wide-awake, forward-thrust head that investigates the field of perception. In the case of these head-oriented people a portion of lively caution is also involved.

People who constantly look down at the ground while walking are particularly cautious. They check the terrain before

Despite the long stride and the head thrust actively forward, the drawn-in chest shows this man's lack of vitality (see p. 87).

The backs of the hands turned forward indicate that this man will not reveal his intentions and feelings (see p. 88).

they set foot on it. They tend to leave their thoughts in the past, only trust steps that have already been tested, and only do what they are already familiar with and are able to do—no risk at any price.

A chest pushed forward reveals an ambitious person who always wants to achieve more than he has so far, irrespective of how high he has risen. When one watches him, one has the impression that he is running ahead of himself, but his legs are always trying to catch up. He never has any time,

because he normally takes on more than he can do, and naturally also has no time for minor matters—that's what one has employees for.

A person who draws back his chest while walking is a person who is not willing. His upper body holds him back behind his feet and follows him reluctantly. For him, life is a battle one has to endure, but only out of necessity. If the chest really caves in, the signal is absolutely clear: I am passive, I do not fight, and everything oppresses me. A sagging upper body

The long, active stride of a man with long-range objectives—enterprising, daring (see p. 89)!

A man who likes to be seen—a little peacock.

always reminds me of a serving cart transporting a head from one place to another. This body has great difficulty in getting the head to move. If the man is told he should do something, he will probably first react with the question: Why me and not someone else? If one insists, he drags himself along under protest.

Hands are for "handling," for action. Brisk movement of the hands while walking shows open-mindedness and willingness. In a natural walk, the hands hang straight down from the shoulders with the planes of the palms parallel to the direction of movement. If the back of the hand is turned forward, it forces an unnatural swivelling motion that hides the palms. Such people hide their intentions, and one does not know what their next step will be: Either they are not prepared to act immediately, or they do not want to reveal their intentions. If one hand hangs lifelessly alongside the body, it is an attempt to block the activity of that side—emotion on the left, reason on the right. The same thing happens when one hand is drawn up toward the chest.

Shoulders that deviate from the centre line with a slight sideways turn and show "a narrow edge," so to speak, remind one—not without reason—of the posture of a boxer who wants to offer as little contact surface as possible. Such people avoid confrontations and evade problems and difficulties. And one more peculiarity: People who find it difficult to make decisions have a rolling gait, where the body sways from side to side like a duck. They have to weigh at length the pros and cons between their feelings and their reason.

The Step

The foot and toe of a resolute person point straight forward: The energy is turned in the direction of the goal as if it were running on tracks. We can quickly explain the importance of the foot position through an image: One simply has to imagine the line of the foot lengthened by a ski. If one turns the toes inward, it slows down every motion—a snowplough. If we turn the toes outward, all the energy goes up in smoke and we fall on our face. Foot position signals exactly the same thing.

If someone walks with his toes pointing in, he is putting on the brakes. We do not know why, but he is braking. And if the upper body exhibits a corresponding position—caved-in chest, shoulders rounded, bowed head—it signals clearly the passive reserve of a taciturn person. He is introverted, and it is difficult to communicate with him. If this person now opens his chest, a conflict arises in his body. The upper part of his body indicates his willingness to receive and exchange information, but when it actually comes to going ahead, something blocks him. His willingness to communicate freely is greater than his ability to do so, and the person finds it difficult to get past this contradiction. He exerts an enormous amount of energy to surmount the obstacle presented by his inward-pointed toes, and it is very doubtful whether he will succeed. The cause can be emotional, in which the foot position is merely an expression of this barrier; but the physical state can just as easily retroact on the inner state of mind and trigger the block.

If the toes point outward, energy is also wasted. One wishes to go forward, but the legs transmit the energy sideways, and the body needs more power to reach its goal. I call this the "wasteful walk." The person would like to appear purposeful, but his body simultaneously clearly expresses that it is inclined and willing to be distracted, to be pulled hither and thither. Of course, there are combinations and variations here, too. For instance, if only the left foot conspicuously turns outward, one can conclude that despite all concrete purposefulness, this person is very open to emotional influences and will risk stepping out of bounds at some time.

When one takes long strides, one places the centre of gravity far forward and assumes a considerable risk in balance. A person who takes long strides thinks big, in broad economic trends, and also takes risks in order to achieve a lot in a short time. Small steps, details, and meticulousness irritate him, make him feel restricted and cramped. Negotiations with people who attach importance to minor matters make him impatient; they inhibit his momentum.

Small steps mean safety above all: Do not rush things, examine everything carefully. This walk is often coupled with a pulling back of the head and a rigid chest posture. If a person who takes small steps is forced to take large ones, he feels uneasy and becomes insecure and nervous. Better to take small, hurried but cautious steps—steady does it!—than to take a bold leap over the risks.

The "peacock walk" puts the body and the person on display. It is pointedly slow, because the onlooker should have time to observe and admire, to recognize the dignity and the burden of responsibility—in short, the measured strides of politicians, judges, priests, actors, people commanding respect.

The broad gait indicates solid ground and seems deliberate rather than clumsy. The energy is employed for a sure step rather than for rapid coverage of ground. One often sees this in people who move on uneven and difficult terrain, like farmers, mountain climbers, or sailors.

The narrow walk is the opposite of this. One foot pushes in front of the other, as if one were walking on a tightrope. It not only expresses insecurity and instability, but also vacillation between reason and feelings. Many women get into the habit of walking like this because it emphasizes the pelvic motion arising from the narrow course taken by the feet. Apart from the intended erotic attraction, and apart from awakening a man's protective instincts, it also gives him the impression he can easily conquer this frail creature because her obvious instability makes her seem so insecure.

Foot Movements

One must already have developed a sharpened perception of the general picture before one can notice such nuances as the movement of the foot while walking. In the ideal picture of a relaxed walk, the sole of the foot rolls rhythmically along the ground. Every deviation from this is a signal.

If the back foot pushes away from the ground at the last moment, with the toes and the ball of the foot like those of a cross-country racer in order to give the whole body a decisive thrust forward, it is a sign of concealed ambition in a normal walk. In negotiations such people will, at the last moment, start a hard battle unexpectedly and try to wangle something for themselves.

If the foot, just before it is set down, tries to achieve a longer step through a swinging movement from the knee, one should expect this person nonchalantly or impertinently to grab another slice of the cake for himself at any time—an impudent pup, so to speak, who always snatches another bite.

If, on the other hand, the foot is pulled back a little just before it touches the ground, it indicates a person who pretends to be more open and generous than he is in fact capable of being.

If the foot hesitates parallel to the ground and then is set down flat without rolling, it suggests a person who is extremely cautious and very distrustful.

If the heel of the foot is set down firmly, if the ball of the foot is pulled up before it rolls, this slows down the movement and diminishes the momentum of the step. Here, ambition is greater than courage. With such a person one has to expect that he will start something with great energy, then put on the brakes at a critical moment. The same thing obtains when the toes of the forward-striding foot are turned up at the last moment before rolling, just as the landing flaps on an airplane have a braking effect before touchdown.

People who would like to look taller, or fear that their inner greatness has not yet been discovered, like to boost their image a little by bouncing up onto their toes again. (In contrast, others constantly flex their knees and act as if they wanted to make themselves smaller. But that is a closely related type and woe betide anyone who takes this understatement seriously. The fact is, such a person's self-assessment is merely using a different kind of mimicry.)

A person who seems to walk on his toes shows he has little contact with reality, with the ground on which he should be standing. He signals caution and uncertainty, does not want to bother anyone. But that is a deceptive signal and often leads to misunderstandings. What about women who look as if they were walking on their toes, barefoot, or a shoe fashion that achieves the same long-legged effect with pointed high heels, and forces the wearer to walk with dainty steps?

If we can talk about distinctive feminine and masculine ways of walking, then the difference is determined less by biological features of the anatomy of man and woman than by cultural standardization and social mores that have set strict rules of behaviour. Starting with childhood, the roles of man and woman are impressed on us and learned. The man, in accordance with his biological function as an intruder and aggressor, is to be seen as the protagonist of power. Therefore, any form of posture or movement on wide-spread legs with long steps that cover a lot of ground is "masculine."

In contrast, for the biologically receptive woman as the inferior sex, a way of walking was ascribed that signals reserve and insecurity through small steps, close together, and is at the same time given the attribute of gracefulness. This applies particularly to women from the "upper classes," in which the sexually provocative walk which emphasises breast and pelvic motion has been cultivated since the nineteenth century. In the

This way of embracing and collecting oneself is the expression of inner concentration and security.

If a woman sits with her legs apart like this, it is a gesture of invitation; if a man does it, it is showing off (see p. 108).

lower social classes this custom of the attractive "narrow-track" walk found no use or was, so to speak, merely put on as Sunday-best behaviour by young girls. Normally the woman of the people moved in a way which was appropriate for their jobs or necessitated by their work. A mother of six in a basement room, a washerwoman, or a maid simply could not afford the dainty, mincing steps of refined ladies. These women walked with steady and not very nimble steps, a "masculine" walk.

Since the middle of this century women in most countries have fought for and got equal rights with men, and thus the pressure of many sex-oriented conventions has been relieved. The fashion of wearing corsets is long forgotten, and more comfortable clothing now leads to a more natural way of walking. One walks differently in jeans and tennis shoes than in high-heeled shoes, and young women in particular have adopted "masculine" patterns of behaviour as a conscious sign of their claims to emancipation. So, on one hand, the battlefronts are no longer so clearly defined. On the other, the stereotypes have not been entirely removed and can be used at any time to revive preconceptions. The things that do not change are the biological signals. A man who sits with his legs apart is flaunting his virility and thus achieves the effect of showing off. If a woman does the same, she opens her pelvic region and gives the impression of being receptive and inviting, which does not look like showing off, but is criticized as indecent, provocative, or shameless, depending on circumstances. And if a man takes small, narrow steps—a "feminine" walk, as instilled conventions come into play again—he is often suspected of weakness, affectation, latent homosexuality.

Sitting

Sitting is a body posture that gives the organism a chance to relax and takes the weight off the feet. Of course there are limits because, above all, the spine still has to continue its supporting function. Complete relaxation of all limbs and muscles is possible only when lying down. But when a person is sitting, we can still see the degree of relaxation in the position and conduct of the various parts of the body. Without constant strain on the total muscle tone, the sitting body is capable of continuing activities, of operating with a wide range of movements and gestures, of giving an abundance of signals that run through almost the entire code of social interchange. In short, sitting is an ideal position for interactive communication.

The rival is excluded from the conversation with small movements of the arm and shoulder . . .

Sitting is a firm spatial position and certain relationships between two or more people can be established through their positioning to one another. This "seating code" has much to do with the order of rank and the territorial claims of the people concerned, and therefore we will have to examine some of the basic characteristics and what they indicate.

Seating Orders

The distance between seated people is also an expression of their greater or smaller personal distances.

If a person is sitting with a group, but there is more space around him than there is between the others, this can be interpreted in several ways. If this space is filled with respect, so to speak, he is surely someone who has more power, a higher rank than the others. If there is an atmosphere of friendly

inattentiveness, he is probably a newcomer to the group. If, on the other hand, he is pointedly avoided, it is a sign of his being "cast out." A position at the edge of the group at a conspicuous distance from the others indicates either aloofness on the part of the others or neutrality of the person concerned. Sitting directly opposite signifies either superior power—be it through a formalized claim as, for instance, in the case of a chairman of a meeting—or an opposing point of view.

The height of the seat also expresses the rank and status of the person who has "taken up his seat" on it. A king's throne is not only larger but, above all, higher than all the other seats around it—so high that no one standing nearby towers over the eye level of the seated monarch. Charlemagne once symbolically settled the power struggle between church and state in this way, when he had his throne in the Aachen Cathedral built so high that no representative from Rome could sit higher. Today such symbols are handled more subtly, and often the softness of the upholstery or the height of the back of

. . . and she takes her revenge by turning a cold shoulder and cutting off the other's line of communication.

the chair have to replace what one cannot democratically assert by raising the seat. But we all know what the boss's chair looks like.

Proximity of seats to one another allows for more intimate contact and shows familiarity. Equals or subordinate groups like to move close together and dispense with territorial distance. By doing this they gain warmth, protection, security, and demonstrate solidarity. When they are sitting in a circle, this unity against the outside is particularly obvious, but even sitting in a line represents the solidarity of their way of looking at things and dealing with them, as opposed to an outsider's. One can see this not only at conference tables but also in cafes, among couples in love. Sitting close together gives them the opportunity to touch affectionately, and at the same time this line emphasises their common front against everyone around. They exchange

These people form a conversation group in which each of them is facing the others.

feelings and experiences and between times play the role of voyeurs, and gossip and chat about the passersby.

Sitting face to face, gazing into each other's eyes, means that each is totally absorbed in the other. This undivided attention can be either object- or emotion-oriented. In the case of loving couples, it means that each is giving the other his undivided emotional attention, even at the cost of physical exchange of affection. It signals self-control and the desire to find each other. Maybe a quarrel, a ''face-off,'' preceded this. At negotiations this seating position simply means: We are going to confront each other on this matter, and find the common point in our respective interests. Every movement of the shoulders that deviates from the parallel line of these fronts then signals in detail a ''turning away'' from specific arguments or suggestions.

Sitting at a corner—in other words usually at a ninety-

When the man directs his attention to one girl, the other feels excluded and draws the man's glance back to herself with a soliciting gesture toward her hair. He promptly opens up toward her again.

Sitting next to each other like this is a sign of intimacy and a common front against others.

degree angle, but close together—establishes a greater latitude of possible patterns of behaviour. On one hand, one avoids the danger of unintentional inflexibility, which can easily arise out of a face to face position, and on the other hand one retains the possibility of direct contact through physical touching without demonstrating total unanimity (sitting in a line) or affection (looking into each other's eyes). In addition, one has the chance to concentrate on one's own thoughts and feelings or create diversions by turning to other subjects or people, because in this position each accepts that the other will also look straight ahead from time to time, and that means past him, or away from him. In short, the seating position in a corner creates a very flexible atmosphere for conversation, which is open to many variations. It is preferred by individualists—by independent or self-willed people—who love a free exchange of ideas and want to stick to their own line without necessarily giving up the possibility of direct contact and closeness to one another.

I could also call corner seating the "democratic seating order," one that can be illustrated with one or two examples. A civil servant certainly feels most at ease behind his office desk. The public, men and women, come to him one after another, and he arbitrates according to his governmental mandate and official function. He's a big wheel, no matter who comes to him; he personifies power and authority—a person commanding respect. But this tendency toward face-to-face seating orders has changed remarkably during the last few decades. Nowadays, the citizen coming for advice usually sits to one side, at a right angle to the civil servant's desk, and thus the intimidating frontal character of this official meeting is toned down. Nevertheless, the civil servant retains his territory of authority: He can use the working zone in front of him and next to us without seeming offensive, can leaf through his papers and read them without aggravating the confrontation with us—because when doing so he turns his glance away from us, in order to ascertain

When sitting face to face, looking into each other's eyes, each can give the other his undivided attention.

something, and not downward to scrutinize us. Such nuances are extremely important, although we are seldom conscious of them. If I was sitting opposite him and he looked down at my personal file or my tax forms, it would be as if he was looking in the direction of my genital zone, my hidden private area. And I would surely consider this to be impertinence, blackmail, or provocation.

Or take the example of a secretary who has been called in to take dictation. Usually she prefers to sit at the corner of the desk. She can see the boss and can take down the text without confrontation; he can dictate his pertinent information without being distracted from the point of concentration in front of him.

When we use the term seating order, we seldom think of a round table. A round table is equivalent to a circle and is supposed to denote the equality of the participants. We see this on television, usually in the United Nations or U.N.E.S.C.O., Eastern or Western economic summits, or O.P.E.C. However, experience has taught us that at such conferences it is not at all a matter of people of equal rank meeting, but that power and status differences become evident even around a round table. That is why protocol favours rectangular tables with a clear head and foot, regardless of whether it is for a conference of a rabbit breeders' association or the discussion of highly political matters.

At such a conference table one sits either (1) in a line, (2) round the corner, (3) face-to-face, or (4) at a distance. And power relationships and groupings are reflected in this order of seating. The point of orientation is always the chairman's seat. The hierarchical structure starts there. Therefore the most honest seating form would actually be a triangle, a power pyramid. But the basic rules apply equally to the rectangle or horseshoe.

The president, the boss, sits at the apex. To his left and right, at the head of the table, are the members of the board, the directors, the most important members of the commercial and technological divisions, or of the staff. The farther they are from the chairman, the smaller their degree of usefulness and importance. Generally the people with the greatest competence sit in a straight line at the head, the experts round the corner, and in the line opposite and increasingly far away are those who are closest to the concrete production and business requirements. This "triangular" structure guarantees power and dominance. Everyone in the descending line is dependent on the decision at the apex, and at the same time there is mutual competition in the facing competitors and the unified groups along the sides of the "triangle." This seating order arises neither out of theory nor because it is prescribed; in the long run it develops on its own through habituation and need for contact.

Here is an example, from my own observations, of how the relationships of the participants to each other can become clear from the seating order. We are dealing with a meeting in which four men took part. They sat at a rectangular table as shown on the diagram.

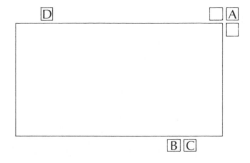

The conversation was mainly carried on by B and C, who together brought arguments against A. A replied energetically and often negatively. D sat there passively most of the time, and only occasionally and very cautiously made a comment after he had first briefly glanced at B and C. The picture that I had already formed from the seating order was subsequently confirmed by the people who took part.

Of course A was the director. His seat at the corner gave him dominance over the table, and also the best view. He sat there in an open posture, his hands on the backs of the two adjacent chairs, so that no one could sit next to him. B and C belonged to middle management; A's provocative posture and domineering sitting position itself compelled their unified line against the director. D, who had kept away from this front line, was a technical expert; his business colleagues' corporate questions and professional rivalry did not concern his specialized position. Before each of his comments he made eye contact with B and C to assure them of his loyalty; yet he was not prepared to join their unified line. Rather, he wanted to avoid a confrontation. He kept at a respectful distance from the director, which was appropriate to his status; he naturally could not take up a comparable corner position, because that would have been a challenge.

It is obvious that this meeting could not be productive. Fronts and differences were fixed from the outset by the seating order. After I had analysed this and commented on it, the seating order was changed, and thus the formation of hierarchical fronts was removed. The meeting soon became more relaxed, and agreement was possible.

The way a person sits expresses his individuality and inner state of mind but also is subject to external circumstances such as lack of time and, of course, direct stimuli of the specific situation, to which one reacts with changes in body posture.

Ways of Sitting

First this applies to the utilization of the surface one sits on. If someone sits on the whole surface with the full weight of his body, he is stating: I am entitled to this, I will stay for a while and it won't be easy to get rid of me.

If someone cautiously sits on the edge of the chair, his centre of gravity remains in front, directly above the balls of his feet, and he can get up at any time. In this way he may be indicating that he does not have much time and wants to leave at once. This "being on the go" can, however, also signal his willingness to help the host at any time, and submit to his wishes. From this point it is only a small step to insecurity: One is afraid of taking up too much time, and is ready to be dismissed at once.

One often sees women sitting on the edge of a chair or seat in this way, but one has to note a slight variation in this case. By sitting in this way women are able to cross their legs, keeping them parallel and slanting to one side, and thus they lengthen the line of the leg. This is not only an erotic signal, it also looks aesthetic. In this position the big toe lies sideways to the ground, and the soles are turned away from it: Thus the signal "no time" or "at your service" is eliminated because the woman cannot get up quickly. Another advantage: The legs, stretched to one side, do not give any support to the body balance, so that the upper body has to be kept erect, which shows off feminine attributes—the shoulders, collar bones, breasts—to their best advantage. Advertising psychologists highly favour this way of sitting in their models.

If a person sits on only half a chair, as if he wanted to leave enough space for someone else, he is lacking in self-assurance. He probably also breathes sparingly, so as to leave enough oxygen for others. These people sacrifice themselves for others and see their reason for living in serving those others. Yet they are constantly tormented by guilt feelings.

A person who limply drops into the chair in such a way that his whole body seems to disintegrate and we fear total collapse, is either very exhausted or really lacks inner stability, strength, direction, and willpower.

In many countries, young people in particular have adopted the American custom of sitting on a reversed chair with the back of it like a shield or barrier in front of the body. There is a large dose of insecurity behind this attempt to be sloppy and casual. Such a person is hiding, seeking protection and cover.

If someone leans back and rocks the chair to and fro on its back legs, using the balls of his feet, he is withdrawing into the position of an observer. He has formed his opinion, perhaps

An aesthetic sight and an erotic signal: The extended slanting line of the legs emphasises ease and grace.

stated it, and now is waiting for the next stimulus before he joins in the conversation again. Then he stops rocking, perhaps even leans forward, and thus draws attention to himself. A very self-assured, slightly conceited person.

A person who sits on the arm of a chair—perhaps even an occupied one—demonstrates great familiarity and sometimes a little too much supremacy. He would like to dominate the group—from above—effortlessly or casually, and set the theme.

When we receive an unpleasant stimulus that we

would like to get rid of quickly, or that actually drives us away, our body often reacts by briefly lifting up off the seat surface and instantly sinking back again. It is a very short, usually unconscious movement of intent, which one can see best in a still-frame on a video recorder—otherwise most people won't believe it happens. An explanation given in my seminars is that the reason for it was the uncomfortable seat. This, in fact, could be the reason, but the immediate impulse for such a slight lifting movement is certainly an unpleasant stimulus. It determines the moment the movement will be made. A man is sitting in front of the television screen, his muscles have begun to ache, but the football game is tremendously exciting, and he does not move from his spot. A kick—it misses. A cry of disappointment, a short lift of the body, a reason to leave; but the game goes on, and our spectator sinks back in his chair.

The posture of the upper body can be interpreted the same way sitting as standing—erect indicates vitality, sunken indicates passivity, a depressive nature. If one leans toward one's partner, it of course shows interest; if one leans back, one also withdraws in spirit. Things become interesting when the signals contradict one another: A person says yes, and simultaneously leans back. He is dissociating himself from his own words, and the body signal is the more important one! A boss who reluctantly gives his approval after a long discussion, and simultaneously sinks back against the back of his chair, is unequivocally saying: O.K., that's the way you want it, but you won't get any help from me. That's it! If he does not lean back until after he has said yes, he is confirming his approval.

Sitting permits a whole range of variations in the foot and leg positions because these limbs have very little or no weight on them. One can lock the ankles behind one another: that is, as if one were holding something back that has not yet been said, or should not be said. But it also shows inner unresolved tension: The poor man is in danger of tripping himself up.

A person who entwines his feet round the legs of a chair is a different matter altogether: No one will ever succeed in getting him away from his standpoint; he will cling to it till doomsday.

People who want to get away internally start to make walking movements with their feet, they slide to and fro, tap their heels. A person who lifts the sole of his foot off the ground, perhaps lays his feet sideways on his insteps, or stretches the feet forward is, on one hand, increasing his territory and well-being; on the other he is signalling that he does not want to grapple

Ways of sitting (left to right)

Legs crossed in a relaxed manner do not always indicate open-mindedness. They can also show degrees of reserve.

The openly casual sitting position demonstrates familiarity; the stretched leg thrusts forward and indicates the claim for broader territory.

The head avoids the direct line of confrontation, and while the open chest posture and broad sitting position show self-assurance, the horizontal shin bone forms a protective barrier.

The feet entwine around the chair leg: You will not get me away from here, this is my position!

The double-locked legs and the cramped shoulders reveal inner tension and inflexibility.

He briefly lifts his body, shifting his position: He feels uncomfortable and would like to leave.

with the firm foundation of reality. And a person who pushes his feet in front of him with a braking movement also puts on the brakes internally, sets up barriers.

Crossed legs supply us with a lot of specific information. Actually, this is quite simply a practical movement and posture, because it strengthens the muscles in the buttocks and the small of the back, and makes it easier to sit for a long time. But crossed legs shows not only increased tension but also subtleties of a relationship. If the person's upper thigh is turned away when he crosses his legs, this movement of intent also signals turning away in the direction of the upper leg. If two people are sitting next to each other in such a way that the toes of their crossed legs are pointing toward each other, they form a circular intention: a sign of seeking contact, affection, and harmony. The opposite position—toes turned away—indicates differences and dissociation. But if several people are sitting next to each other in a line, and all of them have the same leg, right or left, crossed over the other, it clearly shows a high degree of solidarity.

A person with his legs crossed is sitting opposite

The legs of all three women are crossed in the same direction and show their harmony. The man closes the group with his countermovement and forms an intimate circle with the woman next to him.

another who has his legs apart. If his legs are crossed in such a way that his toe points directly at the genitals of the person opposite, he is expressing aggression. The threat is increased if this foot also starts to swing up and down, as if he wanted to kick the other between the legs. At the same time, one must bear in mind that every kicking movement while a person is seated is a reaction to unacceptable stimuli. From this symbolism it becomes apparent that wide-spread legs, the masculine flaunting behaviour showing off virility, are often considered to be a provocation and challenge, and rouse aggression. That is why I find two variations of this comfortable leg position worth noting, because in them this provocation is avoided. Americans, more often than Europeans, sit with their legs apart in such a way that the ankle of one foot rests at a right angle on the knee of the other. That is a casually flaunting and apparently open position, in which, however, the transverse position of the shin forms a barrier—simultaneously conveying protection and retraction of the provocation. The other way of removing the affront from this posture is to conceal it by resting one's lower arms on one's thighs and folding one's hands between one's legs.

The two women form an intimate circle. By crossing his legs in the opposite direction, the man acknowledges that despite his interest he is excluded from the circle.

When women sit with their knees together, they are conforming to the convention of restraint and protection of their chastity. If a woman is morally very apprehensive, a second protection is often added to this: She puts her purse on her lap. And if both feet are placed ankle to ankle, the posture of the "good child" is complete. Serious inhibitions, insecurity, and fear are often hidden behind this conventional perfection. I will give an example from my own experience.

The woman was sitting there, her legs straight as a ramrod, feet parallel, knees together, hands in her lap, a firm voice; the perfect picture of the well-brought-up lady of great self-assurance. She seemed to be proud of everything: the business success she and her husband had achieved together, her three children; she loved to cook, did the housework, and also "menial" work in the office. In short: perfect. She was attending the seminar so that no one could say that she had not done everything in her power for the business. I suggested that with all those accomplishments she seemed to be following the

Showing off: Sitting with legs spread wide apart flaunts his virility.

rules of her upbringing, which forced her to fulfill expectations; that she was not driven by enjoyment and self-assurance, but by a sense of duty. This confused her. She mentioned that her son had graduated from high school, and she made a braking movement with her foot while saying it. I reacted to this signal, inquired about him. Serious family problems were revealed. Her son had set his heart on studying medicine, but he had been meant to take over the business and she bitterly reproached him for not reciprocating properly—in other words, with a sense of duty.

Sitting with one's legs stretched out indicates relaxation—a posture that one assumes more freely in one's leisure time, and when sitting on even ground. If the knees are pulled up and the hands propped up behind, one is building a wall. If, on the other hand, the arms are clasped around the knees, and pull the upper body forward, as if against a balustrade, this is a sign of composure and concentrated attention.

Squatting on one's heels or kneeling is a gesture of humility and submission as a social signal. This meaning becomes evident in numerous gestures and ritual forms. One forces someone to his knees, one begs for help on one's knees. In Catholic penitential processions one approaches the shrine on one's knees, in Islam one prays on one's knees, and in the Far East bowing and sitting on one's knees is still a ritualized form of humility.

The Chest and Breathing

The rib cage surrounds the two sources of power in our bodies, the heart and the lungs. The lungs, through the process of breathing, supply us with vital oxygen. The muscular power of the heart pumps the blood saturated with oxygen to every cell in the body. The interaction of these two power plants supplies us with activity, vitality, vigor. It is surely quite obvious that the flexibility and movement of the rib cage, the habitat of these organs, will also reciprocally influence and indicate their activity and dynamics. Relaxed, strong inhaling and exhaling gives us a feeling of freedom and unimpeded joie de vivre. A rigid chest and shallow breathing also restrict and tone down our emotions. If we keep ourselves short of air and then let it out, we slip into a passive state. If we take air in with expanded lungs, we get ourselves into an active, enterprising state of mind.

This is a conscious accentuation, because normally we breathe through the movement of the diaphragm. When the muscles relax, we automatically breathe in, and this amount of oxygen is sufficient to live. But not for more intense action. To do the latter, one has to consciously take in air, and this happens through the movement of the rib cage. In its turn, this air strengthens and stabilizes the flexible middle part of our body between pelvis and chest, the waist, from which our body's central power output radiates. Its free mobility around the central axis is supported by strong stomach and back muscles. It also helps us to endure hard blows, and we can also increase the load capacity of the spine by breathing in and expanding the rib cage.

Therefore, as long as we do not become resigned from the outset and forego vigorous action, we can say: Every action begins with breathing in. Our chest rises when we switch to activity. We can also see this in the person we are talking to: He breathes in, and is about to get going. If, on the other hand, he is going to yield, he takes a short breath and lets it out again in a resigned way—darn! I can't do anything about that. We should draw conclusions from these behavioural signals. If we can see from the way the other person breathes that he wants to take the initiative, we should give him the opportunity to do so. He will feel better, and he now knows what he wants to say, and can thereby give us information that is important to him and to us at the same time. One should never block anyone who takes this first step; one should shorten one's own sentence, and let him speak. And if he announces his resignation by slowly breathing out, we should be fair, and by toning down our own activity give him the opportunity to regain his composure. If we do not, we will not get much more out of the conversation, apart from a confirmation of our own dominance.

The strength and vitality of our most important tools, our arms and hands, also depend on the active capabilities of our chest. When we are breathing out, their ability to act is limited—vigorous action requires the intake of air, and energy is instantly activated.

We have already talked about some signals of chest posture. When I expand my chest, I indicate my preparedness for activity, confrontation, or aggression. This has its dangers and easily leads to misunderstandings.

When the doorbell rings and a very good friend is standing there with his chest puffed up, your first thought probably is: Well, maybe something's wrong with him. But he continues to walk around or to sit like that, and gradually you begin to feel uneasy. Maybe he does not even know it, but despite all friendliness, this posture in fact signals: "Attack!" You feel threatened, and it will certainly not be a cozy evening.

With some types—"jocks," "great guys," "windbags," and the "life of the party"—the puffed-up chest has become a part of their bearing. Perhaps such a person is actually a perfectly nice guy and cannot understand why people keep away from him. But he should draw conclusions from it, and friends could gently help him. Our body is the glove of our soul. At some point this assumed or adopted permanent behaviour (perhaps he is merely trying to pluck up his courage!) colours his mental attitude. A change in his body behaviour would also change his mental state, or bring it back into harmony.

And finally, an expanded chest is a promise of erotic activity, not only in women. Men, too, do this as a part of showing off, and in it one can still recognize the demonstration against one's rival and the signal to the woman he is courting: I am strong and vigorous. How seriously this should be taken can best be described by the story of the man who comes to the swimming pool with springy steps and puffed-up chest: Well, where are the girls today? There are none. Whereupon his chest collapses, he stops sucking in his stomach, and he says: Thank God!

Head and Neck

In our heads we carry all the sense organs—from aural to oral—that provide us with information, as well as the brain, the central organ of storage and decision-making. A parable from the Far East describes the head's relationship to the neck. A man and a woman were arguing as to who had what to say. The man asserted: I am the head, and I make the decisions. And the woman replied: I am only the neck, but I move you wherever I want to.

If you imagine the head as a radar antenna, naturally its receptivity depends on the flexibility of the neck that moves it. Therefore a very mobile neck reveals a person who is determined to receive a lot of information, is open to every incoming stimulus and offer of communication, and is ready to react to this flow of information. If you want to stop the flow of information and concentrate on one direction, you merely have to block the neck.

To ensure its mobility, the neck has to stand free. But it only has weakly developed muscles to protect it from blows, assaults, and attacks of any kind. Therefore vital organs like arteries and respiratory tracts are very vulnerable and difficult to defend. The neck is "laid bare." There are two ways of

The hand moves protectively to the exposed neck in order to ensure a safe moment of reflection.

protecting it. You can draw up your shoulders and protect the sides of the neck. Or you can bend your head forward and protect your throat. After all, the skull is harder than the neck.

Therefore any way of raising one's shoulders or lowering one's chin is a form of defence. It can be a moment of uncertainty in which I say: I don't know! For this moment I go into a protective position and raise my shoulders. I drop my shoulders again when I decide that the matter in question is not worth being defended. If I continue to think about it and want to keep my options open, I keep my shoulders raised and my chin down.

Baring the sides of the neck is a signal well established by behavioural science. When predatory animals capture their prey, they lunge for the neck because the victim's most vulnerable point is here, and the vital nerve is exposed. Even in contests of rivalry among animals of the same species, the neck is the target, the weak spot. This fact, reversed, led to a gesture of submission. When we want to express submission, trust, or surrender, we openly present the sides of the neck and thus signal that we will not fight. If we want to listen free of intentions and feelings of confrontation, we show it by bending our head to one side, and exposing our neck. In a loving relationship and in love play this gesture is one of the most unmistakable signs. A woman smooths back her hair with one hand and waits for the response with her head to one side. A tender kiss on her exposed neck gives the expected response: I will not betray your trust.

If we are talking to someone, listening to him, and we put our head to one side, we show trust and we take in what he wants to say. As soon as we dislike something—it annoys us, goes against the grain—our head returns to the central line: What did he mean by that? As a result, the other person can see that at this point he has given offense, aroused confrontation, protest. Perhaps all he has to do is make a correction, supply more information, or perhaps he has to change his standpoint or accept a conflict.

It is an entirely different matter if the throat, instead of the side of the neck, is laid bare. In this case the chin and head go upward in the direct line of confrontation, and the neck is exposed at the front. But we call this position "nose in the air," or haughty. It announces: I am confronting you, but I am not afraid. If you jump at my throat, I will react quicker. In other words, a challenge. If someone runs around with his head raised, pointing upward from the centre, it always has the effect of being provocative and arrogant.

I once watched an Italian waiter in a first-class restaurant. He was obviously excellently trained, and perfect in the performance of his job. But he had a small problem. He held his nose in the air. When someone ordered spaghetti vongole, which was not on the menu, and the waiter asked whether he would like something else instead, he got the curt answer: Then I won't have anything. When he promptly brought to a guest a fork that had been forgotten when the table was laid, the customer flinched. Within twenty minutes there was a trace of annoyance at every table. Yet the man was actually doing nothing wrong. He just held his nose too high, and therefore the guests felt they were being treated condescendingly and were offended. In that kind of job, such an attitude is of course particularly bad, because everyone expects a certain amount of deference, and deference cannot be given with one's nose in the air. On the other hand, the waiter was probably convinced that his guests were terribly aggressive and did not know what good service was. He was not conscious of the fact that he was merely getting the feedback from his provocative head position.

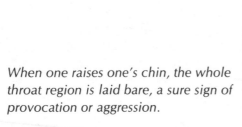

When one raises one's chin, the whole throat region is laid bare, a sure sign of provocation or aggression.

One often comes across the opinion that small people suffer from an especially strong need for recognition and therefore walk around with their noses in the air. This is another instance in which one has to beware of precipitate judgements and take several factors into consideration. Naturally the assumption of "snootiness" applies as much to small people as it does to tall ones, and they seem provocative if they walk around with their noses constantly in the air. But we often get this impression only because a taller person is standing opposite them, so they have to look up. If you sit down with them, you will soon see whether that is their normal head posture. On the other hand, it is just as well to understand that when small people must constantly look upward, it is not pleasant because it automatically forms an up-down relationship. This can be avoided by simply increasing the distance between the two people: The distance moderates the angle of vision and levels out the difference in size. But there is also a counterreaction in people of short stature: They step up particularly close to the other person. In this way they are trying to demonstrate: You do not impress me by your size—I am intruding into your territory, and yet have no fear of your superiority. This is called the Napoleon complex, and it does not necessarily convey arrogance. It can also reveal self-assurance or defiance. Incidentally, extremely tall people have the opposite problem: Their size embarrasses them. They try to compensate for their height and thus take on a very passive attitude. Their chest caves in, their arms hang loosely by their sides, and their movements are inhibited because they are afraid of the tremendous effect of these long limbs. Six feet are quite enough, they do not want to attract more attention, and so they make themselves narrow and docile.

We are born with the shape of our face; similarities to relatives are set by the genetic code. Yet this face looks different because of its structure, its expression, its mimicry. Over the years one's view of life, experiences, and inner state of mind stamp its individuality, which is recognized by the people around us as our identity, and deviations from the basic form reflect our temporary mood. The muscles of the face are very flexible and offer a wide range of emotional expressions. The ability to experience strongly depends not only on the mobility of the chest, but just as much on the elasticity of the cheeks, which give form to emotions and moods. Every vigorous and joyful impulse makes the muscles rise, and when our spirits sink and the joy vanishes, our expression is pulled downward; the energy flow drops. Expressionless faces seem cold and insensitive. Either this person is incapable of intense feelings, or he is afraid of experiences, or he is trying to hide their effect because it is not proper to express one's emotions. If someone organizes his life as if he had planned it on a calculator, so that everything follows a safe course, he has to suppress his feelings anyway, and the rigidity of his plan can be seen in the immobility of his face.

Within the limits of predetermined, developed, or impeded elasticity, we can consciously activate our facial muscles to form an expression that sends signals to others. This can be anything from emphasising a spontaneous feeling all the way to outright mimicry. Our ability to imitate allows us to show whatever mimicry is appropriate to or demanded by the social rules. To a child who is playing we show a different face from the one we show a bank manager. A priest certainly has a different expression at a wedding than at a funeral. And occasionally a diplomat gets used to a neutral mask that also obscures his inner life.

Facial expression results from a combination and interplay of the face's individual parts—though this can often become a counterplay that reveals contradictions. Therefore we have to discuss these means of expression individually, so as to recognize what they are saying; but we must not make the mistake of believing that by themselves they give us the whole picture. It is their interaction that allows us to form an assessment.

The Eyes

The expression of the eyes is achieved through the movement of the muscles around the eye and the eyes themselves, through the intensity of the look, through the degree of vitality in the gleam of the eyes, through the size of the pupils, and through the either relaxed or stiff position of the neck muscles.

When analysing the expression of the pupils, one has to remember that first of all they react purely physiologically to lighting conditions. They contract when there is a bright light and dilate when there is little light, so that we can see better. But the pupils react similarly to emotions. They dilate when the person sees something he desires, something he finds pleasant or is interested in. One's stream of consciousness also gives rise to this effect: When one is concentrating on someone or something, the pupils dilate. Since the dilation of the pupils is connected with a positive feeling, we find people with large pupils more likable, more attractive, as we believe we are the cause of the reaction. Women discovered this long ago, and

Wide open eye contact with different effects: normal and dilated pupils.

have made use of it. In ancient times they used eyedrops of belladonna, an extract from deadly nightshade. Belladonna contains atropine, which dilates the pupil.

Eyes are treacherous, in the positive as well as in the negative sense. Professional gamblers use tinted glasses to keep from giving themselves away, because their pupils dilate when they get a good hand. It works the other way around as well. When intense emotional tension is expressed through the dilation of the pupils, the person we turn to often unconsciously reacts with the same signal—the windows to the soul are opened. The reverse conclusion is, of course, equally correct. When we receive negative or repulsive impressions, or entertain hostile thoughts, our pupils contract.

An intent stare straight ahead with tensed neck muscles—a stare intended to focus on the "bull's eye"—is a clear signal: I am confronting you, I am pinpointing this issue. This prolonged look contains threat and warning; even when critically contemplating something, there is the reservation to

In confined territory—for instance in an elevator—the eyes always search for a distracting focal point, so as to avoid confrontation with the other person . . .

make a negative decision, to reject someone. An intent stare is always a measuring of strength. Who has forgotten the children's game of outstaring one another: The one who looks away first loses. This sensation of evaluation pursues us throughout our lives, when we are caught watching someone and turn away our eyes.

Noticing another person can always be done only by direct eye contact; however, the length and intensity of the look give the signal whether a territorial battle will take place or whether a relationship can develop because this fight is declined. Then the brief glance wanders away and interrupts the confrontation. This ritual is repeated every time two people meet. If they already know each other, this interchange of glances starts their conversation. During the conversation, many kinds of eye contact follow, depending on the statements made and the situation. But at the end, or when they are saying goodbye, this ritual glance is again exchanged.

Among strangers who pass each other at close range on the street and are not otherwise distracted, this contact is also

made. The physical proximity forces one to notice the other, even if neither has any intention of communicating further. The brief exchange of glances, however indifferent it is, also signals: I have noticed you and decline to fight. The same happens when someone enters an elevator or a train compartment. Brief contact is unavoidable, but more is not necessary; it would be considered irritating or intrusive, even embarrassing to oneself. And therefore, with unbelievable interest one stares at the floor indicator in the elevator, or one studies one's fingernails, or the advertisements, and in a train one stares out of the window.

      However, if this ritual glance is not observed, the other person feels ''overlooked,'' and hurt, as if we had said: You have no rights at all, you don't exist for me! This is true even in a close relationship. A husband who reads his paper in the morning and answers his wife's questions without raising his eyes is in for trouble. He doesn't understand what the problem is, because he did answer—but that is not enough. He refused to exchange the ritual glance that is genetically programmed, and therefore his wife quite justifiably feels ignored in her right to

. . . but this always preceded by brief eye contact, with which one signals that one has noticed the other, and declines to fight.

The lowered eyelids show submissive subordination and the bared sides of the neck show trust.

exist, and feels treated as if she were a piece of furniture.

There are relatively strict rules as to the length of the direct glance, but they are different in every cultural group. In Western civilisation the ritual glance lasts from two to four seconds among people who do not know each other; in intimate relations, depending on the situation, it is either shorter or considerably longer. In this context a man and a woman, if they like each other, exchange much longer glances than is normally the case among men. In contrast, in Mediterranean and Arabic countries eye contact among men is much longer. Asians on the other hand look into each other's eyes only briefly, and then their glance wanders up and down between the eyes and the level of the neck in order to assure themselves of the feedback. Africans often look away altogether during a conversation, and do not take up eye contact again until the end, in order to assess the reaction.

If someone wants to convince us of something, and is not sure of his arguments, he usually tries to transfix us with his

The wide open eyes and open mouth signal expectation and willingness to receive information.

eyes, and thus does not turn them away for a second. He wants to force us to concentrate on him. In fact he achieves a very different reaction, because within five minutes, we are no longer listening to what he is saying, but are totally absorbed in meeting the challenge of his glance: We get ready for battle. Therefore, even in an intense conversation, one should always give the other person a chance to look away, to digest the information, and to put his own thoughts in order. Then he, of his own accord, will return his eyes to us, ready to receive more information again.

Occasionally I am asked whether one really looks into both eyes, just into one, or between the eyes. The question itself shows how awkwardly we handle our body language. If I look between someone's eyes, at the ridge of his nose, I transfix him, and he is forced to figure out whether I am confronting or ignoring him. It is not making contact, and no communication can develop from it, because the other person is confused and justifiably notices that I am not revealing my feelings to him at all. One also does not look into one eye (this would have a similar effect), one looks into both eyes, into the "face," and at the same time our eyes wander in smaller or greater deviations.

The deep, affectionate glance is exchanged between mother and child, or between lovers, or it appears when watching a situation that arouses loving feelings. The eye muscles are relaxed, the head bends to one side, the neck is soft and supple. A dreamy look causes a similar posture, but the eyes have a rapt expression; the gaze seems to be turned inward or into the distance. Loving couples can sit next to each other this way for hours. They look lovingly into each other's eyes, see the world around them as if through a mist, do not say a word, and in the end they say: It was a terrific evening. The emotion and tenderness in the language of their eyes is the best form of communication for them.

Normally our glance is directed in a straight line from the head and eyes to the object we are watching, and a change in the direction of the glance comes more from a movement of the neck than from the movement of the eyeball. As long as nothing unusual happens, the eyes, too, do not react in a noticeable way. But as soon as something happens that breaks through the customary perception, the muscles open up and the eyes widen, as if they were enlarging their focal point. The muscles retain this tension in order to prevent the eyes from closing due to other external stimuli. The result is calm attention. This reaction will always occur whenever an unusual event is perceived. An abrupt movement, a sudden noise, an unexpected meeting, fright, or surprise. The eyes are opened wide, demand more information, more *extensive* information.

The moment of surprise triggers parallel reactions in the body that can easily be seen by trying out an experiment. If, while walking, you suddenly open your eyes wide, your foot will slow down at that same moment, your neck will stiffen. The reason: The eyes function as an alarm signal that warns and protects the whole system. When they widen suddenly, they signal something unusual, and that could mean danger. Legs and neck are blocked, the entire concentration of the body is directed at the triggering moment—any movement now could be wrong. If a closer inspection is reassuring, the eyes return to their normal position, and the movement resumes. This link is so synchronous that we can determine the exact instant when our eye widened from the moment at which our step faltered.

Generally, of course, we will be more likely to adapt our behaviour to a change in the "blink of the eye," since we are, after all, looking into the other person's face. If at some

point during the conversation his eyes widen, we have a signal that always means: I would like more information. The reasons why he wants it can vary. He did not quite understand something. He heard something unusual and is curious. He has discovered a weak or dangerous point and wants to protect himself.

A concrete example demonstrates what helpful ideas and means for communication this signal—the widening of the eyes—can open up for us if we take note of it. In an informal conversation after signing a contract, the salesman tells his customer what great difficulties his company is having with their new fleet of trucks. And at this point the customer looks up wide-eyed. Why? It could be that he himself wants to buy the same make of trucks, and therefore wants to know more about them. But maybe he is wondering whether his products will be delivered on time, since the salesman is having transportation problems. Or he thought of comparable problems in his own company, which have nothing to do with this conversation.

The mixed reaction: I half believe you, but I am suspicious and want to know more.

The concentrated look: I am focussing on one specific point.

Whatever the case, this is important: One must take note of the "wink of the eye" and respond to it. Then, through cautious inquiry, one can find out which assumption is correct, and react with appropriate information.

When the eyes are narrowed, the upper and lower lids drawn together, we signal a desire for information—however, not for elaboration and supplementation, as was the case with widened eyes, but for greater depth and detail. One concentrates on one point, one narrows the focus: The trimmings now are irritating, I want to know the exact details. Of course, one has to be prepared for two possibilities if the other person narrows his eyes. It probably announces a purposeful question: Just a minute, I do understand, but you have to clarify this point. In this case, it is obvious what you have to do. But it can also be that the other person is concentrating on himself at this moment, is searching for the detailed answer in his own mind. In that case, you must leave him in peace. When the expression in his eyes relaxes you will know he has finished his contemplation.

As long as I am looking at someone, I am not only receiving the other person's verbal information but also trying to find out his attitude. Because there can be a contradiction here, too. He tells me something that is quite matter-of-fact or very pleasant, but I see in his face that he does not like it. At this moment, he probably turns his eyes away, breaks off the contact, in order to concentrate on himself. Perhaps he wants to hide something, not disclose a weak point, get his thoughts in order first. He does not want a confrontation and interrupts the flow of information, including information from me to him. It all depends on how long this interruption lasts. If it is brief, and he turns his eyes back to me, I must not press him, and also have to wait if I am talking. When his eyes return to me, his glance says: O.K., I am with it again, and ready to communicate.

If the eye contact is broken off for a longer period of time, there is danger in the delay, danger for the resumption of an exchange of views. The giving of information becomes one-sided, and there is not even anyone to receive it, because the other has figuratively already taken to his heels. He cannot run away with his legs, but he has run away with his eyes. We know this from children, who practice this behaviour quite openly. When we scold them, they look in the direction in which they would like to escape, the direction that draws them. Or we see it in a lecture hall. The speech drags on, and the people gaze out of the window; their eyes start to wander.

If the person one is talking to narrows only one eye, or winks with it, he is signalling suspicion, doubt, half and half: You're withholding half of it. If I wink back, I confirm assent: Agreed, we'll bypass that part. Or maybe a bit more; that is to say, the two of us agree on what has been left unsaid. This signal has very definitely entered the language of gestures in Europe. You narrow one eye and open the other with your forefinger: You can't rip me off, I know better. This can be meant quite nicely, but also very contemptuously.

The eyes move to the side when one does not want to commit oneself. One obtains the information but avoids the confrontation by turning head and eyes away from the direct line of vision. Only the eyes move to the source of the information from time to time—in other words, to the speaker or questioner—but in this position the impression of turning toward someone is only apparent, simulated. As schoolchildren we perfect this technique, because it allows us to obtain information we need from the side, apparently unnoticed. And if there is nothing there, the eyes wander upward—but there is no writing on the wall.

An upward glance always seeks help or assistance from

a higher authority. It happens with the exam student who waits for the redeeming great inspiration, or with the professor who prays for indulgence and compassion for so much stupidity. One turns one's eyes heavenward when one would love to see someone disappear from the face of the earth, and also when one sees the futility of one's own efforts, and gives up one's activity. But even the Lord God is relatively unresponsive.

Looking at the ground and one's toes is a characteristic of people who live on their earlier experiences and shy away from new ones. They think in a conventional way and will only make claims when they are on sure ground: what they have achieved, what successes they have had. New plans and suggestions are eyed with caution and compared with old ones for a long time before they are accepted. New ideas are most likely to make an impression when backed by solid traditions and detailed examination. The antithesis to this type is a person who always looks straight into space. He either lives in the future in an unrealistic dream world, or he bets on future possibilities with great daring and a grand design. There is a continual conflict between these two antithetical characters, both of which are indispensable for the growth and development of social organization and economic adjustment.

By closing our eyes we also cut ourselves off from outside stimuli—that, again, is a generally valid, basic element of human body language. In cats and snakes, the whole body, in fact, completes this feeling: They curl up. Birds bury their heads under their wings. And even many people complete this withdrawal into themselves in their sleep—they put their arm over their head, draw their knees up, curl up for protection. Closing our eyes even when we are awake is a sign of fatigue, exhaustion, or overstrain. The incoming stimuli become too strong, the information swamping us is too voluminous, and we shield our eyes by lowering our lids. It is an unmistakable sign when the person with us briefly closes his eyes and nods while we are talking: Enough information, I understand. But we also close our eyes against truths that hit us hard, and perceptions we do not want to accept: The stimulus is too strong and too unpleasant—we shut it out. Timid people quite often give the impression that they are ready to "close their eyes to reality" at any moment.

The downcast glance is a sign of humility and submissiveness; but this is judged differently in every cultural group. The characteristic feature of Western culture is confrontation. Anyone who does not accept confrontation is, in that culture's eyes, running away from responsibility, and that is negative. He must have a bad conscience, be ashamed, or be lying, otherwise he would stand and face it. In this way humility or submissiveness have come to suggest degradation or self-denial.

In other cultures things are different. In some, for instance, eye-to-eye confrontation is considered to be obtrusive or intrusive. Under the historical and religious conditions of Arab cultures, it is considered insolent and presumptuous if a woman looks straight into the man's eye, and so she keeps her eyes lowered. When she looks up, it is a very strong, individual, intense, and emotional signal.

According to the customs of African cultures, it is impolite to look in the eye a person whom one admires, holds in high esteem, or respects. One looks past him, to one side, when one is talking to him. This is not a sign of submissiveness in the European sense, but a matter of propriety and politeness. It does not express that one feels one is weak, embarrassed, or inferior, but that one is modest, reserved, and retiring. One does not

The defensive look: I disapprove of the matter, and I do not want to see it.

confront another, but prefers to communicate on a level that is freer of conflict.

This also applies to the cultures of the Far East, which are even more difficult for us to understand. Our impression of Japan is one of incredible assimilation, uniformity: identical suits and presentation depending on the occasion, indistinguishable behavioural patterns and rituals. A large part of this impression arises from our arrogance and ignorance, because in fact their behaviour and rituals are extremely differentiated, but according to different rules and forms than ours.

So the same signals can have different values in different cultures, and this is the point when body language becomes a foreign language. As long as one is dealing with basic elements, which have entered the genetic code through biological evolution, the meaning of the signals is generally identical. However, as soon as they have been refined over centuries through cultural and social characteristics, they can have divergent values that we, as strangers, have to handle with care.

The Mouth

We eat with our mouth, appease our hunger, satisfy our appetite. Because of this, our mouth is equipped with sensitive taste organs like gums and a tongue, which supply us with exact information about everything we eat. The reaction becomes visible through the movement of the tongue and mouth-lip muscles. And we also open our mouth and move our lips and tongue when we establish contact with the outer world through speech. How closely these functions are connected in our conceptions can be illustrated by numerous expressions. Hold your tongue! Why don't you open your mouth? He spits out sentences. He's got a loose tongue. She has a glib tongue.

When taking in information, the mouth reacts similarly as when taking in food. When something "too big to chew" comes at us, a weighty "bite" of information, our mouth opens. At moments when we are astonished, surprised, or scared, the flow of information is greater than we can take in and digest at one time. Our lower jaw drops, as if we could increase the inflow of information with our mouths gaping. At the same time our eyes are opened wide. Surely this description conjures up the picture of children watching a magician or a wonderful

Punch and Judy show, incredulous and astonished.

The dropped jaw also has a blocking effect: Our thoughts slow down. Try this yourself: Drop your jaw, and now answer quite quickly: How much is thirteen times seven? You feel you need longer, want to close your mouth so as to concentrate. A person who is overburdened by the world, and can only process reality with difficulty, quite often runs around with his jaw hanging down. If you discover this expression of wondering admiration in an employee, you should not expect too much of him at one time, because despite good intentions he will only take in and execute half of what is demanded of him.

When you receive pleasant taste stimuli, your tongue presses against your gums. This is linked to a sucking reflex. The smacking sound is made when one tries to stimulate the gustatory nerves. And on the other hand, the tongue pushes things we do not like around in the mouth, or out of it. It reacts analogously to secondary stimuli—arguments, thoughts, sensations.

I don't like that: The tongue pushes this impression away.

130

The comment apparently left a bland taste behind: The tongue wipes it from the lips.

Sticking one's tongue out is quite rightly interpreted as a rejection of an insulting intention. "It" does not taste good and does not suit us, we want to get rid of it. In contrast, one runs the tip of one's tongue across one's lips when something tastes good and we enjoy it, as if the tongue wanted to collect the last crumbs of the treat. This is also why running one's tongue slowly across one's lips is received as an erotic signal, which is meant to suggest and stimulate sexual activity. In doing this, one also wets the lips, increases their shine and their sensitivity. If I am deep in thought, digging out thoughts from my memory, my tongue often digs between my teeth as if for scraps of food. And when I bite my tongue, I punish or warn myself: You should not let this comment get out. The man bites back a comment, or bites his tongue rather than say something.

Parting our lips is the first movement that enables us to take something into our mouth, to ingest it. If we like the taste, we pull up the corners of our mouth into a cup shape so that

everything stays in the cup of our mouth and nothing is lost: the "sweet-taste expression."

If we do not like the taste, we pull down the corners of our mouth, so that what has been taken in can run down or out: the "bitter-taste expression."

If it tastes especially sour, our head and the corners of our mouth withdraw in a simultaneous escape movement: the "sour-taste expression."

Crying and screaming are reminiscent of an escape reaction because of the contorted muscles, and the pulled-down corners and gaping mouth remind one of the refusal to take anything in. These actions are often coupled with the unfriendly threatening signal of bared teeth.

Lips that are pressed together state plainly: I do not want to accept it, or say it. This instantly indicates to us that we can expect harsh criticism or a rejection from the other person. A tightly closed mouth is a characteristic feature of people who

That was a nice compliment: The tongue collects the last remnants.

You bite your lip as punishment because you cannot fulfill an expectation.

The corners of the mouth turn down disapprovingly because you do not know something.

Mouth and lips are pressed together: I don't like that, and will not accept it.

Something pleasant: The softly pursed lips and the gentle touch of thumb and fingers suggest a pleasant sensation.

In time, constant emotional states set the expression of the mouth. An embittered grouchy person is easily recognized by the downturned corners of his mouth, and a happy person, who enjoys life like a gourmet, gives his face a radiant sparkle through the upturned corners of his mouth—he simply smiles.

An honest smile is formed through the interaction of eyes and mouth muscles, which also have parallel nervous systems. At the sight of a positive stimulus the eyes widen slightly, seem to gleam, while the receptive mouth takes on the sweet-taste expression in joyful anticipation. This signal develops very early on, when the association between pleasant expectation of food and the sight of the mother is particularly obvious.

Because of its positive value as a signal, the smile became a demonstrative part of the greeting and meeting ritual. If the teeth are bared at the same time—a wide smile—a moment of superiority could be involved: I can bite you, but I won't use my teeth because you rouse pleasant feelings in me. Combined with other emotions and facial movements, this smile can very quickly become "dishonest," insincere—an embittered, cynical, deliberate smile that hides evil intentions. The eyes do not join in the smile, they remain cold, hard, or glitter disturbingly.

The teeth have the task of chewing and crushing what we want to eat into small pieces so we can swallow them, ingest, and digest them. That is a necessary and positive aggression and destruction without which we cannot evaluate foods and incorporate them into our body. An unchewed, gulped chunk of bread is not food for the body, it is a foreign object that the stomach cannot process, responds to with a stomachache, and rejects with much pain: One vomits. Spiritual foods need the same digestive process. One has to reduce them to bite size, bite them off and ingest them bit by bit, continually making them smaller so that we can digest them and integrate them into our system. Information, confrontations, emotions—as they come at us from the outside.

Someone who can bite, who has a bite, is also a person who does not shy away from hard confrontation, and does not swallow hard chunks unchewed or regurgitate them undigested. He faces his tasks and makes them his own. People who do not like to use their teeth, and prefer easily digestible food—sweets and spoon-fed arguments at the trough of easy handouts, cheaply promoted liquid food—should be considered rather indolent and mentally lazy, and unlikely to exert themselves.

This trusting embrace reflects heartfelt joy and the security of belonging.

They expect service and are easily influenced by hard pressure or gentle seduction.

Eating habits give us a lot of information about the characteristics of people. Fast eaters do not taste their food, they swallow it quickly without chewing, and can hardly digest it. They do much the same with information. They snatch it up, gulp it down, and regurgitate it undigested in the form of slogans and catchwords, repetitions and well-known clichés. They can seldom add anything of their own, they spit undigested stuff around, fragmentary, disjointed, because the ideas do not fit together. The dissolving and rebinding effect of one's own thinking, like the enzymes in saliva, is absent.

She and he: a relaxed laugh.

She and he: a coquettish smile.

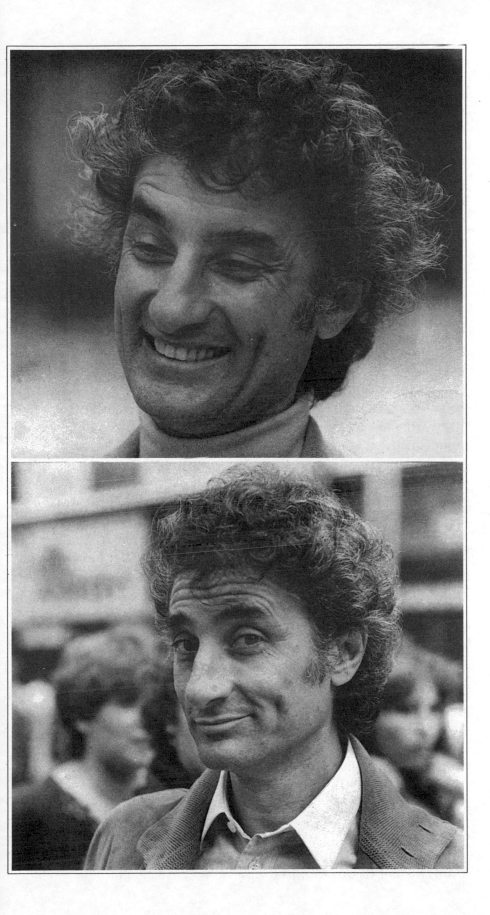

138

Others perform a surgical feat while eating. Very thoroughly and with great relish they dissect every chunk of food on their plate until they have cut out the best pieces, and then carry them to their mouth; they are just as choosy in life. Others constantly find fault with the subject they are operating on: The meal is too hot or too cold, too bland or too salty, too much or too little. In life, too, they find fault with everyone and everything, and presume to have opinions about everyone and everything, yet they are absolutely incapable of intensely enjoying or experiencing anything. One can merely advise these people to eat slowly, chew carefully, to pause from time to time, learn to enjoy. But they are hardly likely to do so, because they are so sure of themselves, or so insecure, that they need to behave in this manner.

Really, observing eating habits is excellently suited to studying behaviour. Over here we have a man who tears the pieces of meat and vegetables from his fork with his teeth one by one—a "snatcher" who is incapable of teamwork and grabs everything for himself. Over there a man is gulping food that is too hot—he cannot and does not want to perceive nuances, he just wants to have the matter over and done with. Over here a man is drowning everything with lots of ketchup, salt, and pepper—every impression has to conform to his preconception of taste.

We should like what we ingest, it should taste good, because we want to make it into an integral part of us. We also identify it as a gift from someone we like: The way to a man's heart is through his stomach. Yet we will also accept a meal that is not particularly good from someone we love. However, under other circumstances we hardly ever eat what we do not like, what does not taste good. It arouses aversion, repulsion, nausea, it revolts us—and our organism repudiates it, spits it out.

We react the same way to nonmaterial stimuli. Comments and actions that we do not want to accept, assaults and insults that we cannot return, situations and fears that we cannot deal with cause us to feel unwell, sick, nauseous. In a state of great excitement we spit out sentences, eject them. We find it difficult to swallow, and sometimes we feel as if our stomach were turning over. We vomit, wet our pants, and in this way at least find physical release. Spiritual and moral stress eases off slowly; but every physical elimination provides release.

One spits on someone in order to repulse him, to show him how disgusting he is, and that he is held in contempt. And one refuses to eat in order to demonstrate disapproval. Children do it; husbands do, too. In the same way we react to disappointments or heartache through our eating habits. They take our appetite away: We do not want to accept the reality. Or we compensate for the grief we have suffered by excessive gorging. Or even more complicated: Out of grief or rage we gorge ourselves, which is fun, and get fat so as to punish the other person ostentatiously—revenge is sweet. As I said: The way one eats is the way one is.

Clenched teeth quite simply give a dogged expression. It is the attitude of not wanting to give, take, or yield. You sink your teeth into something and hold it tightly in silent rage, and do not let go of it even if it is of no real use to you—like a dog with a stick between its teeth. If you meet someone working in this mood—whether it is a housewife ironing, or the man of the house filling out the tax returns—and invite him to go for a walk, he will probably answer with undisguised reproach: Impossible, *you* might be able to afford to do that, but I have to stay with the job. He reproaches you with his own doggedness and pig-headedness.

The nose, the olfactory organ, is not a very mobile body tool, but for that very reason it is capable of giving some remarkable signals. The nostrils are brought into tone and begin to vibrate as soon as we receive an exciting smell, and eventually they react like that in any state of excitement. Very sensuous people—the type to whom one jokingly ascribes "animal instincts"—quite consciously dilate their nostrils in order to receive more sensory information, or to signal their own sensuality. In distending the nostrils the sensitive olfactory cells are opened wide, and therefore, with this movement, we examine what we ingest. When someone is deep in thought, is examining a thought, it is quite often accompanied by a twitch of the nostrils. If there is a bad smell, we wrinkle our noses, and analogously indicate that the matter stinks.

The Hands

The hands are the most sensitive tools and most expressive limbs a human being has. The refinement of their abilities, parallel to the development of the brain, describes the biologic evolution that led to homo sapiens. Whatever the brain thought up or imagined, the hands had to put into action and realize; what they learned and were capable of opened up new possibilities for the brain to shape life. The structure of the forefeet changed in such a way that one of the toes wandered from a position parallel to the others into an opposing one: The human being was capable of holding something between his thumb and forefinger, of grasping it, and the flexibility and sensitivity of these terminal members kept increasing until they became such an incredibly sensitive organ of touch, functioning as a mobile tool, that science and technology have not been able to reconstruct a comparable universal instrument to the present day.

There are approximately 3,900 nerve endings concentrated in one-tenth of a square inch of a child's fingertip, and there are between 1,900 and 2,600 on an adult's. With these fantastic skin antennae one can feel a hair or speck of dust, and differences in thickness down to hundredths of an inch, between thumb and forefinger. The surfaces of our fingers and our palms give us precise information about the structure of a surface, and we take it for granted that through them, without looking, we can distinguish not only between fur and a brush, but also between velvet and silk, artificial fibres and natural ones.

In the past, before machines and appliances took the burden off the capabilities of and demands on our body to such an extent, market women, farmers, or craftsmen could exactly determine weights of one-quarter or three-quarters of an ounce by holding the objects in their hands. And the same hand that can sense the changes in hardness from the resistance of iron when hit with a blacksmith's hammer, and announce it to the brain, whereupon the other hand uses the bellows to increase the heat so that the iron remains soft and pliable—this same hand can, within one second, elicit twelve consecutive notes, on the keys of a piano or strings of a violin, and emphasize this succession through dynamics, rhythm, and feeling! And this hand is not an instrument to which we have to bring objects. By means of the joints of the fingers, hand, arm, and its length, we can reach anything in space, in any direction, moving straight ahead, in gentle lines, swinging curves, wavy lines, round the corner; we can grasp, feel, hold, stroke, push, pull, turn, hit, chop . . .

His expression is one of deep concentration, and the hand holds back a comment until the information has been digested.

The eyebrows drawn together indicate inner concentration, and the hand closes the mouth during the thinking process: Should she say something or not?

When we are considering something, the hand holds back the words.

We grasp for the world in order to grasp it conceptually. Only by getting in touch with it are we assured that it really is as we imagine. Or different. In the latter case getting in touch—and everyone associates a hand movement with this word—forces us to correct our conception.

The importance of the hand lies not only in its precise manipulative and sensing abilities, but in the interaction of the hand and the brain. The capacity and size of the section of our grey matter (cerebral cortex) devoted exclusively to the hand show just how great it is. The thumb and forefinger each claim more than ten times the portion of the cortex than is allocated to the foot, and more than the head with all its sense organs.

The differentiation of the spheres of the brain allows the continuous interplay of sensation and perception on the one hand, and reacting and handling something on the other. "Handling something"—this interrelation between head and hand has a fundamental character in the formation of words and language: to "catch on" or "find gripping," to "grasp" or "hit on" something, "behold" and "underhanded." Many basic abstract terms demonstrate this concrete connection, if one looks closely.

The hand is one of the most important tools of active communication between us and the outside world. We perceive something with our eyes. That gives us a picture and we form an approximate image. Perspective vision allows us to evaluate the size and distance. But we do not get more exact information and true proportions until things are within our reach and we can touch them. We establish contact with them through our hands. We give and take with both hands. If we want to break off this relationship, we pull back our hands. We point out things with our hands, we use them to describe something, and to express our feelings. Considering this abundance of functions and possibilities for communication that our hands have, it becomes evident what a straitjacket is imposed on a man whose upbringing aims at impoverishing movement, at reserved behaviour and holding back. It suppresses the language of his hands and thus takes away one of his most important methods of grasping the world. A person who cannot express himself with his hands, or get to know another with them, sacrifices one of the most important means of communication and restricts his own wealth of emotions.

Our arms move away from our body when we want to touch or grasp something, take it in, or reject it. With this movement we open up the body and take away the protection the arms and hands give it along the sides. So we need to have

When in danger, arms and hands protect the head and neck.

the trust and assurance that nothing can happen to us during such an action. Otherwise we will not move our arms far from the body, so that it can retain its means of defense.

The arms can effectively execute their defensive function in two ways. In active defence the hand, by making a fist, becomes an offensive weapon, and using the arm as a lever it can reach the enemy. It can also seize or strike out in other ways. Its strength is increased by the way we breathe and tense the back-chest muscles. An attack can be averted, or intrusiveness blocked, with outstretched arms—pressure is being exerted. Or with a swing of the arm we throw something away from us, toward a target.

In defensive protection the arms try to shelter the body and stay close to it by crossing over the chest or the head. This protective movement is often accompanied by raised shoulders.

Because of their angularity and hardness, the elbows are good weapons of defence and symbolize resistance. In children—but also in adults who scold them—one often sees this position: legs apart, hands planted on the hips, and elbows turned threateningly outward. Also, in conversation, if one expects a verbal attack from a certain side one pulls up one's elbows.

If, during a conversation, a person leans back, places his hands behind his head with elbows pointing out to the sides, this is a very definite signal. He has said all he is going to, the subject is closed as far as he is concerned. Now he is defending his position with his elbows. Of course, in this casual expression—after all the body is opened wide and without defence—there is also a dose of arrogance: I've already got the solution, but you're sure to need more time before you get it, and anyway, my position is unassailable.

The actual "el-bow" is formed by propping oneself on one's hands in preparation for getting up; also when weak or exhausted we support our hip with our elbow. In both cases it is a matter of protection in a situation where we are particularly susceptible and vulnerable. Perhaps that also applies to pin-up girls who, by resting their hand on their hip, raise their breast, and in doing so point their elbow backward, protecting the rear.

The movement of the upper arms deserves special attention. The active emotional energy that flows through our chest mobilizes a motor energy that is converted into the movement of the upper arm. Openly emotional people move the upper arms away from the body and in this way express their natural trust, their willingness to communicate, exchange information: I give—wide open gesture; you give—wide swing of the hand towards oneself. In southern countries—France, Italy, Greece—people talk with wide open arms. In the north, and particularly in the industrial countries of Central Europe and in the British Isles, the upper arms are held close to the body and move very little. There are upper-class families and fashionable boarding schools where the children and pupils are given books to hold under their arms while eating, so that they will learn well-bred and affected manners. The upper arms may not be moved away from the body; that is not proper. One has to be disciplined, and thus one gives nothing; one inhibits one's movements, and thereby suppresses one's feelings. Such upbringing blocks a person and forces him into a corset of rules and regulations. He becomes a true product of social restraints. Emotions are taboo.

When moving freely we draw or describe a wide circle of relationships around us. With rigid upper arms one can at best make the movements of marionettes: a little to the front, more in the direction of momentum than radius of reach, a little to the right and left, more rejecting than grasping for something. No broad circle; instead, a reduced rectangle, blinkers, shortened field of vision. And one becomes accustomed to this, is afraid of attracting attention and showing feelings; shies away from great expenditure of movement or feelings; considers people who do not have this constraint and reserve, who do not permit blinkers or chains to be put on them, to be crazy and extreme.

Let us assume that such a person is the product of good English upbringing, from Eton or Harrow and then a good university. And now, according to family tradition, he becomes a second generation politician—naturally conservative. He has to convince people—a relatively large number, pretty much strangers—and give election speeches, make an impression. But unless he possesses rhetorical charisma that, let's face it, has been pretty rare since the times of Demosthenes, he will not succeed with closed arms, he will not come across, he will not go down well. He has to open his arms and make expansive gestures in order to embrace them all, to draw them to him. For this reason he takes a course in body language, in nonverbal communication. But it is not enough to learn a few tricks. One has to become totally involved, and this demands strength of mind, examining and being aware of one's own behaviour, its limitations and their causes. This man is doing it for political reasons, for his career. He has to try to acquire free, open behaviour that runs counter to his whole upbringing.

The meaning and creative power of body language is much more natural to other peoples; but it is not exactly the rule to bring up children with a dream career in mind. There is the Jewish story of the mother who went for a walk with her two children and was asked how old they were. She replied, "The doctor is five, and the lawyer seven."

In all cultural groups where the upper arm remains pinned to the body, the lower arm and wrist have to assume the expression of movement—and nothing much happens. The rigid position of the upper arms forces experiences to be suppressed and reduces the exchange of contacts with the surroundings. By the way, even here we can observe individual nuances according to left-right priorities. A person who keeps his left upper arm pressed against his body is particularly frugal in expressing or exchanging feelings, lacks personal contacts, and—to compensate for this—is often cynical. A rigid right upper arm indicates problems in making decisions in concrete and practical situations.

The hands can only make contact through the movement of the arms. Therefore arms and hands that hang passively or "as if paralyzed" at the sides of the body indicate

I do not know how to get a handle on this matter.

A polite refusal: The open hand and the bared side of the neck are signals of trust.

I will make you an open offer!

A curt refusal: The hand slices dominantly downward, head and upper body dodge defensively.

that someone does not want to act or communicate, possibly even feels paralyzed. Resignation and great disappointment are also expressed by dropping one's hands. If the hands open up, they commence some activity. Therefore, from this we can see whether our partner is in a passive phase or whether he is ready to act.

We have already mentioned that folding one's arms across one's chest is a defensive form of expression. Yet one must also observe other signals. If the shoulders are raised at the same time, and the chin is drawn down, the body is cowering, and this is certainly a defencive posture. However, if these accompanying phenomena are not present when the arms are folded across the chest, it is more likely to be a blocking of activity. Because, as we said, the flow of activity radiates from the chest and sets the arms in motion. A very active person who is used to handling things himself, and now passes on a task, has to check his own zest for action at this moment. He folds his arms and with this gesture says: Now it's your turn. As long as neck and head remain turned toward us, relaxed and attentive, this person is not closing himself off from us, but merely from his own activity. Audiences often assume this position, and that is a very positive sign. They take things in with their minds and senses, and increase their ability to concentrate by blocking their activity. If they want to, or should, take a position, they are sure to unfold their arms. If they do not, one has to motivate them to do so through an appropriate stimulus, because only then will they be ready to take an active part.

When arms are drawn back they also indicate that they are withdrawing from handling anything themselves. If a person holds his arms behind his back constantly or for a long period of time, this indicates that he passively accepts that the person he is with should do as he likes, or even more: the wish not to do anything himself. Yet this by no means rules out intellectual activity. This person could merely be deep in his own thoughts, and is considering what should be done. It is also possible that this person has something to say about everything and will inundate us with advice in a couple of moments, but he will not lift a finger to put the theory into fact. Many bosses are like this, because it is the typical posture of people who issue orders.

One small additional movement makes this characteristic feature absolutely unambiguous: One hand tightly clasps the other by the wrist, either behind the back or over the stomach. This is the position of a person who calmly watches others working, or curiously observes an accident, without the slightest intention of getting involved or doing anything about it himself, and pretends it has nothing to do with him.

When the arms are jerked sharply upward, almost invariably the fingers are spread apart: One recoils from something and does not want to touch it, wants to drop it, reject it, because the stimulus is much too sharp. This gesture signals either literally or figuratively playing with fire, or dealing with a repulsive matter.

Our arms expand the gestures of our hands. Yet in our cultural circles it is considered unseemly, and in some societies even impolite, to talk with our hands. Nevertheless, we do it. A North German student attending a seminar once assured me, with absolute conviction, that he did not talk with his hands at all. A video recorder immediately proved that while he was talking, not more than fifteen seconds elapsed when he did not move a hand or lift a finger. However, he did keep his upper arms rigidly against his body. A person who immobilizes his hands is a very monotonous being, because it is absolutely impossible to convey involvement in any information without the hands participating in some way. In this context there are two basic positions: the open hand and the covering hand.

An open hand displays its palm. The palm is at least twice as sensitive as the back of the hand: a person who shows the sensitive side of his hand offers us trust and shows his willingness to act amicably and cooperatively, because he does not cover up or hide his sensitivity and feelings. It is the gesture of free give and take, a gesture that also recurs in the iconography of pictures of saints, in the motifs of blessing, intercessory prayer, and presentation of gifts. A person who hands over a present, a letter, or any object with his open or cupped hand seems pleasant, he awakens trust and meets with calm reactions. During a conversation, when one presents arguments with an open hand, it signals readiness to accept counterarguments and removes the intention of confrontation. A person who offers an argument, a suggestion, an impression, or an invitation with an open hand, invites an exchange and allows the other to decide freely. The open hand signals respect for the other person, and the offer of a balanced interrelationship. When one has put all one's cards on the table, one is "open-handed." Nothing is being concealed.

The covering hand turns the sensitive palm downward and the back of the hand up or against the other person; it protects the sensitive side from the outside world. Hands that constantly turn their backs toward the other person during a conversation either protect feelings (due to insecurity) or they are trying to conceal something. People with this habit are difficult

150

to negotiate with. They cover up their intentions and are seldom willing to compromise. Quite often they set themselves boundaries of principle, just as their hands build a wall between the argument and the other person. Hands that rest on a table, on the arms of a chair, or on one's thighs also signal the same tendency to cover up—even more intensely as if they are hidden under a table.

A downward movement with a covered hand suppresses an imaginary countermovement, it offsets a counterweight, makes a counterargument more difficult. This downward movement is a dominant movement, and we will now look at that in more detail.

Someone is standing at a lectern and pushes down applause or catcalls with his hands: He wants to calm down and pacify the crowd, but only in order to be able to dominate it more effectively. If he turns his palms upward in the same gesture, it is by no means an open gesture, but a suggestive one, which is meant to give emphasis to his statements, and call forth

Suspicion: The hands build a wall to hide what one is doing.

agreement and loud applause. It admittedly contains the signal: I will raise you onto a pedestal—but with the suggestion: Raise me onto one!

Or think of a boss who points out a typing error, an overlooked memorandum, or an unsatisfactorily completed piece of work to his secretary or an employee with his jabbing forefinger, holding the back of his hand towards the other person. This emphatic gesture precludes any objection or defence: The man simply asserts his dominant position. All he needs to do is to answer a courageous counterargument with a sweeping motion through the air, the back of his hand toward the employee, pushing it away contemptuously, shooting it down: This is a high-handed insult.

We are usually very quick to notice if someone handles us with condescension, even if we do not consciously connect it to the signals that make this posture clear to us. Someone offers us his hand with a solemn downward movement, sweeping his hand through the air in an arc, the back of his hand toward us,

Pressure generates counterpressure: The response to the dominantly outstretched forefinger is a countermovement with the back of the hand.

152

as if we were meant to kiss it—a conceited guy. He is in fact imitating a gesture with which temporal or spiritual rulers offered their hand—wearing the ring symbolizing their power—to their subjects or followers of the faith to kiss. Or someone slaps us on the shoulder in jovial recognition: Well done! Jovial means "like Jupiter," the father of the gods, and that is exactly how he means it, a bit high and mighty: Well done—almost as well as I could have done it.

All these are dominance movements, and we make several of them ourselves occasionally, unwittingly. They instantly trigger feelings of confrontation, protest, aggression, even when the signals are not taken in consciously, because this reaction is genetically anchored in us. The marriage partner's reaction is sullen or angry, the friend is annoyed and sour, the employee reacts with a bad mood—antagonism and reduction in productivity. A kind of repressed punitive action can be the result: Our secretary overlooks an important appointment, our wife forgets a telephone call. Therefore, beware of downward

This friendly recognition is highly ambiguous. The dominant pat on the shoulder from above simultaneously contains a warning: Stay down, just where you are!

dominance movements with the covered hand! Small changes in behaviour can have a great positive effect. If instead of patting someone's shoulder from above, I do it from the side, on his arm or back, then I am turning my open hand to him and this enveloping gesture also intimates an embrace. This kind of recognition will certainly not be considered jovial shoulder-slapping, but friendly approval.

We close our hand to grasp or hold something. We make the same movement during a conversation or when thinking, when we want to grasp a thought or get a handle on a matter, or to demonstrate that we have done so.

The hand looks for a hold when we lose our balance or feel uncertain. Whether the hand closes round the bowl of a pipe, a lighter, a sturdy glass, or a purse, an attentive observer can register this moment in which a reference point is sought and found.

A very strong and constant threat triggers the need to cling to something, particularly in insecure people, in the same

This is friendly recognition that intimates an embrace. Of course, this hand movement can also manipulate by steering a guest toward his seat.

The archetype of clinging evolved
from an embrace.

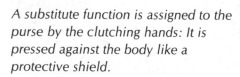

A substitute function is assigned to the
purse by the clutching hands: It is
pressed against the body like a
protective shield.

Here the hands clutch the arms of the
chair as a reaction to a possibly
threatening remark.

way that a baby ape clings to its mother's fur. The object can be the back of a chair or the edge of a table, even one's own wrist pressed hard against the body; one seeks a refuge to which one can cling. In the figurative sense one can also cling to titles, positions, habits, phrases, and ideologies from which one dare not break away for fear of falling into a vacuum.

Where people are concerned the clawlike hand is actually a symbolic weapon, even though women do achieve considerable effect by scratching, using their sharp nails and dexterity to compensate for the strength they lack. However, the tensed clawlike hand is also used by men as a symbolic threatening gesture. It signals aggressive feelings that can augment to hate and raging fury, a mental tension that can lead to fanaticism.

The fist is a natural weapon that everyone uses as a matter of course, not only in order literally to punch others in the face or ribs. We shake it threateningly, we slam it emphatically or forcefully on the table, or at least wave it through the air with a brief elegant movement, since—let's face it—hitting the table is a sign of bad manners and lack of self-control.

A clenched fist always sends out an aggressive stimulus and is correspondingly answered by the other person, even if neither is conscious of it. Once in role-playing we took a hypothetical situation in which a building contractor had exceeded the agreed costs and was submitting the actual costs to his employer. After beating around the bush for a while the contractor declared that he was prepared to accept an offer— and clenched his fists. That *was* a positive concession, and the employer claimed, when the exercise was over, that he had not noticed that the contractor had clenched his fists. But the employer's response was spontaneous—hopefully, out of court! The video recorder then showed him that in fact he had not failed to notice the contractor's clenched fist and had reacted aggressively toward it. Because this fists also signals: I am ready to fight for this thing or idea. Before we respond to it with aggression—I am at least as strong as you—we should try to find some means of communication and talk about it. But in order to do this one first has to recognize the signal and be conscious of it!

A caressing hand attempts to sense the form, surface structure, and temperature of a specific object by touching it gently, and thus establishes the experience of an interrelationship to it. The sensation, and the feeling gained through it, are very different from intellectual perception. Angora fur is angora fur, a rose is a rose, but observing them with one's

156

Even this small movement with the forefinger, the "know-it-all," can be dominant and inhibit the other person.

The words can sound very understanding and accommodating— but the clenched fists reveal the aggressive undertone.

A hybrid: the left ("emotion") hand shows cooperativeness, while the clenched right ("logic") hand indicates a suppressed conflict.

The "pistol" is to be interpreted both as a gesture of defence and as a warning.

eyes or under the microscope calls forth in us a very different impression than touching them with our hand. We perceive them—but we do not experience them. They arouse the longing to touch them, because only then is our desire for true experience, direct feeling, satisfied. So, during a conversation that touches and affects us, we try to increase our sensitivity by caressing our palm with the tips of our fingers or by rolling a pencil between our thumb and forefinger. By doing this we stimulate our nerve endings and sharpen our senses, increase our sensitivity.

Turning to or leaning toward someone is connected with the desire to sense the other more intensely and feel his emotions. This gives rise to tenderness, the gentle and sensitive caressing of one's partner. We come into gentle contact with him through the touch of the skin and simultaneously create a relaxed, compliant atmosphere through the soothing rhythm of the caress. In a moment of solitude, when we feel lonely, we grant ourselves the same sensations through caressing. By stroking an object I also convey to another person my desire for tenderness.

Describing (drawing a picture of) something with one's hands—that is a very appropriate word formation. Long before people discovered the possibility of recording something with symbols (some sort of writing) and passing it on to others, they used signs with their hands to emphasise their information and to communicate with one another better. Using the movements of their hands, they drew shapes, impressions, and feelings, and thus described them more precisely and sensually than it is possible to do through the abstract form of a word alone. Signs with one's hands still have this auxiliary and supplementary significance and effect, even though our powers of speech are much more highly developed. Sometimes a movement of the hand is enough for us to understand instantly.

If someone wants to describe a spiral staircase, he will immediately make an upward spiral movement with his thumb and forefinger. If he wants to describe an attractive woman or a handsome man, we instantly know what graphic description to expect. If he wants to close a topic for good, he will draw a horizontal line with his flat hand. If, during a meeting, he wants to signal that it is high time to eat, he will either point to his mouth with his fingers or pat his stomach with the flat of his hand.

Or imagine how a boss explains certain working procedures to his employees. With both hands he "builds" a succession of walls with spaces in between: Each procedure is to be separate from the next and then dealt with step by step. With a diagonal movement his hand describes upward steps: One has to start at the bottom and then progress upward in steps. He indicates a frame with his hands to each of his employees, and denotes the area of work they have been assigned. Then, with a suggestive movement, he presses his thumb against the top joint of his forefinger: They should take particular trouble with this detail. And finally he describes a circle with both hands, or puts his hands together as if he were holding a ball: That's how he will get a handle on the whole project. Such scenes can be developed into a pantomime solely through the movement of the hands, and anyone watching will understand the whole process even without words.

A person who pushes something away with his open hands signals that he wants to keep something at arm's length. There is a very notable and convincing example for this. During the Vietnam War, President Nixon held a television conference during which he tried to pacify the protesting youth with grand promises. Literally: I promise you you will get everything you want—and while saying this, he very noticeably pushed his hands forward. There was a flagrant contradiction between the verbal promise and the nonverbal statement, which revealed his inner attitude. Because, in fact, it meant that he was only willing to give what was absolutely necessary to keep the protests and the rebellious youth off his back; in this way Nixon denied his own credibility. Under the correct assumption that he would give way only under pressure, the demonstrations continued.

This gesture of pushing something away is not only made by your hands with imaginary objects in the air. One also pushes things away on the desk—papers one does not want to deal with, an innocent ashtray, or an empty coffee cup—when one is under inner pressure, wants to push away a suggestion or refuse responsibility.

We use the same gesture to rebuff someone who comes too close, who invades our territory, whether it is because he comes physically too close to us, or is too pushy with his questions, or spreads out his papers too much. We push his papers or notebook away a little bit, and signal to him in this way that he should withdraw back behind his own borders. If our hands suddenly begin to tidy the objects on the table it means: The information is too disjointed for me, I first have to put the matter in order.

Our hands can also be attacked by a cleaning quirk. It is a sign of character of people who constantly wipe things off the table top, set things in perfect order, or keep dusting. They

An attempt to get a firm grasp of the subject.

In order to describe something precisely, the thumb and forefinger move in a horizontal position.

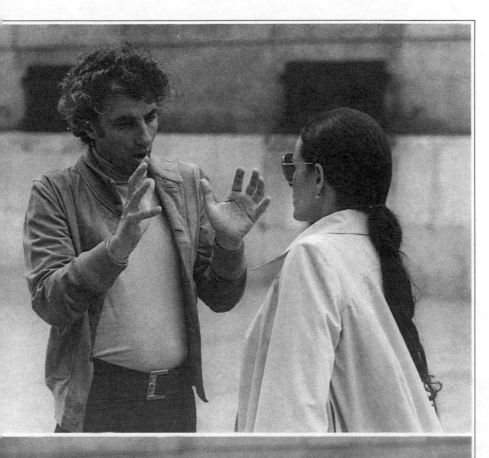

The whole thing is a round, self-contained matter.

One has to keep the things separate: One hand shows the boundary, the other pushes something away.

want everything around them to be nice and tidy and gleam harmoniously, just as they imagine it in their dream world. They have difficulty in dealing with unpleasant things and the hard facts of life; they avoid confrontation with reality.

If, in contrast, someone absent-mindedly or with surprising concentration wipes a crumb from the table or picks some lint off his sleeve, he is probably responding to a disturbing momentary stimulus that he wants to remove or shake off. Or a man comes to his boss with a really good suggestion, and the latter starts to push things away, to polish the table top, and casually tidy up: He is inclined to reject the suggestion since he feels uncomfortable because he really should have thought of it himself. In such an ambivalent situation the employee would have to give his boss the feeling that the boss really was the father of the idea and has the project in hand—otherwise he will reject it.

Movements with both hands emphasise the statement of the open and covered hands—whether I am asking for

The "porcupine" shows his defensive finger tips.

something, greeting someone and embracing him, or protecting myself. I can build a protective wall in front of myself by resting my elbows on something and forming a pyramid either with the "fist in hand" position or by pressing my fingertips together; the position of the fingers indicates increased inner tension. If this pyramid is lowered forward it acts like a keel, the prow of an ice-breaker: The forward-pointing apex rejects, threatens, or attacks the person opposite and the lower arms deflect any assaults or interjections that may come at us.

The pistol: Both forefingers aim forward like a gun barrel, both thumbs are held rigidly upward like the hammer, the rest of the fingers are clasped back like the handle. The aggression of this image is "pistol" clear.

The cogged latch: The fingers are intertwined and loosely interlocked, slightly tensed, and ready to open up to tackle the matter instantly. Greater tension can be seen by the whitening knuckles; the locked position prevents actively taking a hand.

The fingertips seek points of contact.

The fingers point at the palm: I expect to get something.

The hands rub each other: I am contented, I feel great.

Fingers against the forehead: I am trying to stimulate my thoughts.

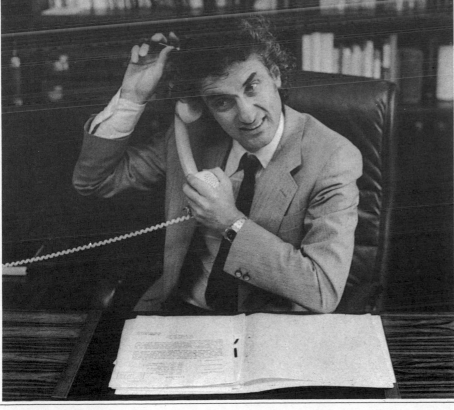

The "substitute finger" scratches the head: I have to decide one way or the other.

The fingers adjust the glasses: I would like to take a closer look at this.

The porcupine: The intertwined fingers spread out and defencively show their tips.

If both hands come together in the shape of a pyramid and the fingertips touch gently and tentatively, it is—like the weighing movement of two open hands—always a search for points of contact, for a balancing of mutual interests, and indicates the willingness to come to an agreement.

We often rub our hands together when we have come to a decision or are ready to get to work. It is as if we were trying to warm our hands so that they can put our plans into action accurately and with feeling. Yet the same gesture can express contentment or spiteful glee: We feel great, and want to savour it completely through increased sensitization.

Similarly the movement of washing one's hands signals relish, but if it continues, it suddenly gives the impression of wringing one's hands: an expression of indecision and helplessness. We scratch our palm with our fingertips: We long

A stroking movement under the nose with the forefinger: this needs careful consideration.

for something, we are itching to do something, we hope to get something.

When we lay our palms diagonally across each other and clasp our fingers around them, the position suggests an embrace. This fatherly gesture is very popular among priests and some sermonizers. The language of this gesture is gentle. It either soothes or it makes the other person angry, because there is no exchange of feeling in it.

Naturally we touch our own body with our hands and fingers primarily to take care of it, clean it, and satisfy immediate needs—in other words, physical functions. We also use our hands to protect the body from overintense physical stimuli: shading our eyes, covering our ears, and the like.

But this is the boundary where touching with one's hands also becomes a communicative signal: Hand on the forehead, hand on the stomach, hand on the heart. And last but not least, touching, particularly with the fingers, serves to

The hand rubs the neck: an uncomfortable situation.

The fingers stimulate the eyepoint on the ear: I would like to see the situation more clearly.

The finger tugs at the collar: I feel cramped.

The hand goes up to the mouth: Just don't say anything out loud!

stimulate certain functions and sensitivities. These are simultaneously identifiable as behavioural signals.

Our hand goes up to our forehead when we remember something; the fingertips tap it when we want to recall a lost thought; they rub our temples when we search for new ones; forehead and eyes sink into our hands when we are exhausted or want to fully concentrate on something. People who wear glasses push them toward their eyes when they want to take a closer look at something. Our fingertips play around our lips when a correct and careful expression has to be found for a complex matter. Our fingers make stroking movements under our nose, above the upper lip when a thought is being subjected to a final scrutiny; they pull at the tip of our nose when a comment misfires or was embarrassing. Our hand goes up to our mouth to block a precipitate remark, and rubs our neck in a disturbing or uncomfortable situation, in order to discreetly protect the head, and to shift the burden from the neck. Our finger slips between neck and collar when we feel cramped and

When we are tired or under strain our fingers block the flow of information by closing our eyes; and by pressing lightly they create a pressure balance.

need more air and space. We take our earlobe between thumb and forefinger in order to increase the keenness of our observation by stimulating the eyepoint, known from acupuncture, and to gain an insight into something or, by gentle stroking, to animate and reward ourselves. We bite our finger to punish ourselves, and chew on our nails when we do not want to swallow reality. . . . This list could go on for pages and be enriched by ever new individual discoveries.

The thumb is the dominant finger—the strongest of all of them in controlled mobility, and the one that makes it possible to grasp things, the one that locks the hand's grip. The thumb's expression always has a dominant character; the thumb "ex-presses." In the Roman Empire the emperor turned his thumb downward to have a gladiator killed, and turned it up when he granted him his life. In aviation today the high sign means everything is O.K., ready for takeoff. The smug petit bourgeois pushes his thumb under his suspenders and pulls them forward while clenching his fists: Here I am, who wants to take me on? This does not happen by chance. Whenever a person tries to monopolize a conversation, or extols himself and his achievements, his thumbs spring up. Admittedly, if such an extremely self-confident person tries to hold back, his hands and fingers are clenched, but his extended thumbs maintain his claim to dominance. Conversely, people who would like to hide away, who are afraid that someone might notice them and expect independent action from them, hide their thumbs by clasping their other fingers around them.

The Fingers

The forefinger is not only the most sensitive finger, it is also the "know-it-all." If we want to indicate a direction or an object, we do so with the whole hand; but if we want to point it out precisely and emphatically, we use our forefinger. The pointing forefinger instructs: I do not merely have a vague idea, I know it precisely and in detail. Knowledge is power, knowing it all is overbearing. We threaten with an outstretched forefinger, we punish ignorance with its whipping movement, and club it down. Since well-mannered people do not point their fingers, they hold a ballpoint pen, their pipe, or their glasses between thumb and bent forefinger as a substitute, and hammer at counterarguments with them. Or they bore for weak points with their forefinger and stab at them as soon as they have discovered them. They can also use the forefinger in combination with the dominant thumb by bending it over the tip of the latter, and then they peck at us or at an object with this pointed beak. People with these kinds of finger habits are usually very unpleasant.

The middle finger is the finger of self-expression. It is the largest among its peers, and thus the symbol of the way we see ourselves: We pay great attention to ourselves and hope others will do the same. If I emphasize the importance of this finger, give it pride of place, or hold it in my other hand, I am signalling the desire for recognition and praise, or I want to talk about my successful achievements. The middle finger and forefinger like to stick together: symbols of knowledge and of the "I."

The extended dominant thumbs demonstrate self-satisfaction.

The fingers set the limit under the pillars of the thumbs: I will make concessions so far, but no further.

The locking of the hands prevents their opening up and brings the thumbs into a dominant position.

The hybrid of an open offer that has limited possibilities.

Hand-play (From left to right)

He holds her hands with a dominant claim—his thumbs are on top.

She signals protest and her own claim by extending her forefinger.

She attempts to get a grasp on the situation, while he, by gently touching his emotion finger, indicates that he is sensitive to what she is saying.

Affection, belonging, loving care are shown in this touch of the hands.

The ring finger is the emotion finger. It is always joined to our "I," and therefore is almost unable to move without the middle finger. It is difficult to say whether one wears the ring there to demonstrate the bond with one's feelings, or whether the symbol of emotion was assigned to the finger because one wears the ring there. Its role is relatively passive.

The little finger is the social finger. It cannot do much but is always present. During the baroque era, aristocratic society developed a codex of elegant behaviour in which the fine movements of the hand played quite an important role. The little finger always had to be kept slightly apart from the rest of the hand. In his fantastic comedy, *Le Bourgeois Gentilhomme*, Moliere describes how the bourgeois social climbers, the nouveau riches, studied this behavioural codex and attempted to be accepted as men of rank and title by emulating it. Some "people of quality" still extend their little finger so high into the air that they nearly poke out others' eyes. Yet a modern refined gentleman holds his little finger quite casually, and has done so

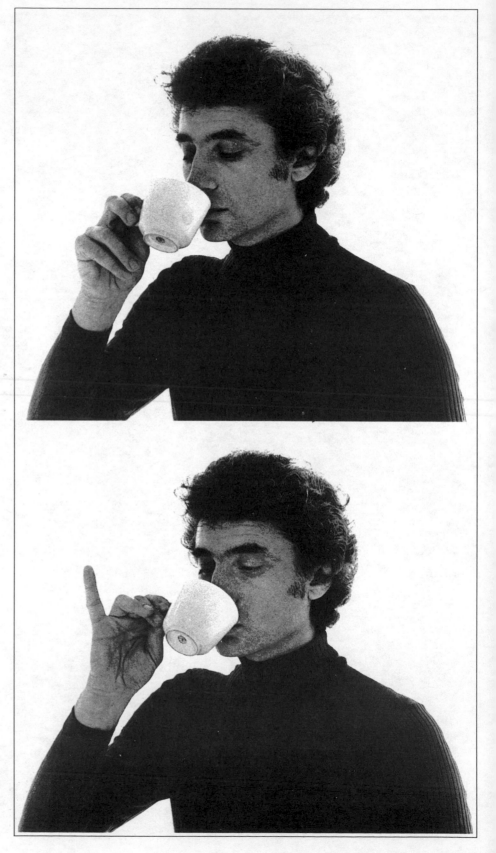

A small movement of the little finger demonstrates a large difference. In the one case the retracted social finger indicates individual understatement.

In the other, the way the little finger is stretched out signals demonstratively: I, too, belong to refined society.

for a long time. In some cultures a long nail on the little finger is still considered to be a status symbol: It shows that one does not have to do any hard work, and belongs to high society.

People who take rules of etiquette very seriously still consider it to be a sign of bad manners when one puts one's hands in one's pockets while talking to someone else, particularly a "higher ranking" person. Luckily most people no longer stick to such rules as slavishly, because in body language this gesture has a very friendly meaning. Putting one's hands in one's pocket simply says that one is not inclined to be particularly active at the moment, and would prefer to have an easy, relaxed conversation—small talk, a few polite or friendly words, nothing of importance. In fact, high-ranking people— and not only Prince Philip or the Prince of Wales—make use of this gesture to create a casual atmosphere and to break down exaggerated barriers. Even a speaker who puts his hand in his pocket signals: Now don't take my position toward you too seriously, we want to have an informal conversation among friends.

Manners

Used and understood correctly, this movement can in fact ease tension. A father is about to lecture his son, and the latter casually puts his hand in his pocket. Now, if Dad is a parent of the old school, worried about his authority, he will probably hit the roof, because young people, subordinates, and underlings are meant to keep a respect-full posture when one is talking to them. And if he is this type, then his dear son will probably be demonstrating defiance and resistance with this gesture. However, if the father is less beset by self-doubts and authoritarian principles of upbringing, then he may recognize an offer in this gesture: O.K., let's talk about it, but don't let's make a big deal of it. And he can clear up the disagreement in a calm, open discussion.

We actually only touch strangers in order to do them a favour or to help them—we lead an old lady across the street, help a child to his feet, and so on. This functional contact respects the bodily taboo and has no other significance. Only with people we know well do we break through this natural

180

The appearance of intimacy is misleading: With her right hand she blocks his, and protects her neck against a possible attack. Not until the embrace is unobstructed does it signal absolute trust.

distance in order to make contact and get closer. We put an arm round their shoulder in a protective gesture, to show friendship and concern. If a person puts his arm around the neck of his partner or a child, it indicates his dominance (which is meant in a friendly way, but is unmistakable) and the subordination and trust of the other, who is forced to expose his vulnerable neck because of this gesture. Touching the head presupposes a particularly high measure of trust because the person being touched exposes this important part of the body with all its sensitive organs. Stroking the head or cheeks, touching eyes or lips, leaning one's head on the other's shoulder—all these statements have many nuances from consolation to tenderness, but they always express great intimacy in the relationship.

The bounds of intimacy are very limited in our

latitudes. In most Mediterranean, Oriental, and Latin American countries there is a much freer, less fearful, and less strained attitude to this kind of touching. The people like to touch one another, and do it often, to show trust and liking; they use their body's means of expression much more naturally. Even between men, gestures of affection and friendship are normal, fond embraces and affectionate touching—which in northern Europe are considered to be exclusively erotic signals and therefore are very quickly misunderstood. If someone draws back from this, a southern European is likely to interpret it as a personal rejection, which was not at all the intention. In fact, this can lead to even more attempts at touching and efforts to make contact because the more temperamental person wants to show his affection at all costs. The behaviour of young people gives us reason to hope

The loving touch of head and lips, the gentle touch of mouth and hands, endearments and affection are part of the ritual of lovers moving from mutual awareness to finding security in each other.

181

that even here, in the cooler north, things are gradually changing and people are learning to deal more freely with the language and expression of the body.

Touching between lovers arises from the desire to become aware of each other, tenderly and with sensitivity to sense one's own emotions in the other. Hand play helps to discover and return the signals and sensitivity, the reaction and reflexes of one's partner, providing support, refuge, and warmth.

A hand on one's lover's hip is a clear signal to the outside world of an intimate relationship. When touching hips first appeared in folk dancing, it was just as daring a development as touching hips in a waltz, because the erotic significance of this contact really cannot be ignored.

Touching lips and tongue, the kiss, is talking and giving at the same time, and suggests the union of the sexual act, which is stimulated by intensifying the love-play by touching the erogenous zones around the breast, thigh, and abdomen. One gives oneself to the other by giving one's body.

This course is preprogrammed by nature and observed as a ritual. If one of the partners omits or skips one of these steps it will be considered as an aggressive advance or intrusiveness. The order of precedence of this preprogramming is different from culture to culture.

There are also "occupational touchers" who are permitted to touch our body familiarly and intimately, something we normally allow only loved ones to do. Doctors and nurses, masseurs and hairdressers cannot do their jobs without putting their hands on their patients, clients, customers, and touching parts of the body we do not normally reveal to a third party. This kind of contact triggers stimuli—that is unavoidable. We try not to react, and to ignore these stimuli by regarding the occupational toucher as a "nonperson" and considering the contact to be a functional procedure. But it is in the nature of stimulus contacts that they give rise to familiarity, and conversations develop accordingly. If one wants to avoid them, one has to take care to keep to a very objective eye contact from the very beginning; otherwise the occupational toucher is irritated, because our behaviour is contrary to his experience, and he is, after all, merely performing his professional tasks. On the other hand the occupational toucher easily and unintentionally becomes the victim of a "legitimized affair." People who suffer from a lack of tenderness and intimate contact, whose need for affection and touching remains unfulfilled, understandably seek compensation for this longing.

"Occupational touchers" like nurses or waitresses are permitted to invade our rigorously protected intimate zone. But in order to keep our distance and avoid intimate contact, we simply ignore them as "nonpersons."

Lonely and old people like to go to doctors more often than really necessary, to entrust themselves to them. Women who feel neglected find their way to a beauty parlor or hairdresser rather often. There they get a little of the gentle touching and recognition they miss. Gymnastics, dancing, acting, and sport also offer skin contact and feelings of security through physical contact.

A person does not feel happy if bodily nearness is withheld from him, and when one has rules of etiquette that make bodily contact more difficult, or make it taboo, no human warmth can develop. We always communicate with one another on two levels, one rational and the other emotional. When only one of them is addressed it is not enough—neither for mutual understanding nor to satisfy our individual needs. The human being is a social animal. However, he also takes care that his invulnerability, his territory, remains inviolate—very few people are allowed to cross these boundaries.

Our secretary, in her role as a functional person, is also permitted to cross the protective zone of our personal territory.

Territorial behaviour is a result of the survival instinct, and is genetically programmed in people, too. We distinguish four territorial zones.

Territorial Behaviour

The first territorial zone is our own body. The second is determined by the distance necessary to defend our body against assault. It is set by the arm length or reach of the person who could harm us. At the same time it is the social zone that is observed when we meet someone, or during a conversation. However, this distance differs in every cultural group. Arabs stand close together, Englishmen farther apart. Crossing this boundary to move closer is considered to be intrusion into the intimate zone; leaving a greater distance is aloofness.

The third territorial zone encompasses the area we need to protect our family or group: apartment or house, farm or village.

The fourth territorial zone is the area we stake out to safeguard our food and livelihood. It used to be the hunting grounds and the agricultural area; today it is more likely to be the section of town and the workplaces where we live and work. Depending on the way we look at things and our interests, this zone can, of course, be more broadly interpreted. As a Viennese, I may look on my city as a territorial zone; as a Swiss, my canton; as a German, my country; as a worker, my factory; as a director, my company; as a politician, the interests of the group I represent. There are many kinds of living space.

I take possession of an area through claim and conquest, and must be able to protect and assert myself against intruders from outside, challengers from within, and my own competitive offspring. I must fight and be on my guard that I am not hurt, because that would weaken my defence and decrease my chances of survival.

So that man can protect his territory, ritual signals have been programmed into his genetic code, which we can classify according to three features:

• fighting signals and showing off
• marking territory
• hierarchical signals and status symbols

Any intrusion into our body against our will is a violation of territory. This applies not only to injuries or rapes, but also to operations or injections without our consent. And to forced feeding.

The good mother who insists on forcing a child to eat, and despite his resistance stuffs the food into his mouth with a spoon, is not a good mother. She is violating the child's territory

The exemplary "good child." However, he is hiding his emotion hand in his pocket and showing his dominant thumb.

and breaking his will. It can lead to this person later not fighting for his rights and considering it a matter of course that adults, superiors, authorities violate his territory, and to his accepting that he is inferior and weak. A mother has to behave the same way as a dentist who wants to get at his patient's filling: He waits until the mouth opens and signals assent. Territorial signals must be respected. One may not force entrance, one has to take the trouble to motivate the other person to cooperate.

Fighting Signals and Showing Off

The first threatening signal among primates is the intent stare. The strength and perseverance of the adversary are assessed from the eye contact and duration of the stare. If they seem overpowering, the wandering gaze signals submission; the one who feels inferior indicates renunciation of further conflict and gives way to the victor, or subordinates himself to his dominance. This also has advantages among animals with social orders. The stronger and most dominant member of the species protects the common territory against attack from outside and enjoys privileges when feeding and mating, which in their turn determine the hierarchical structure of the group and prevent or reduce conflicts among the group members. The weaker enjoys freedom of movement within this hierarchy of rank, and the protection of the stronger within his territory.

If the eye contact does not lead to a clear result, further threat signals are exchanged, which are meant to impress the adversary and persuade him to give in. Even four-legged animals stand up on their hind legs, kick with their hooves, spread their paws; apes drum their fists against their puffed-up chests, show their teeth; cats bare their claws and raise their hackles just as birds do their feathers, and porcupines their quills: Look, this is how strong I am, how big, how dangerous. If these signals and all the showing off do not work, fighting is unavoidable. It ends with the defeat of one of the adversaries, which normally—if it is a battle between members of the same species—is admitted by signals like lowering the head, raising the rear end, exposing neck or throat, or precipitous flight.

Human society is not much different. Territorial conflicts involving physical injury, manslaughter, or murder are

admittedly strictly prohibited by law, and only permitted in self-defence, but even if one excludes criminal acts, there is an abundance of daily aggressions, brawls and fights, which can be attributed to real or imagined territorial violations. And our arsenal of ways to show off—threatening gestures, fighting signals with which we try to intimidate our adversary—is highly stocked.

Yet it all starts the same way as between the rabbit and the snake, or one stag and his rival—eye to eye. One transfixes one's adversary with a stare. The one who looks away has lost it. If we come too close to someone, literally or figuratively, we violate his territory. We know the look he then gives us, and avoid it, look down in embarrassment, and withdraw. And in the gestures and body language that accompany a conflict we recognize many of the signals depicted from the world of animals—we do not really need to describe their modification to human use.

I would like to point out one special human submissive gesture because it has solidified into a conventional posture, and is the result of social conditioning. If someone stands with legs apart and feet firmly planted on the ground, it signals the claim to stable, sufficient ground that he has taken possession of with his body—to territory. On the other hand, standing on a small area indicates the fear of taking up too much space, insecurity, subordination, and the renunciation of territorial claims and fighting. This is exactly the posture that is instilled into good citizens and well-drilled soldiers: feet together and parallel, legs pressed together, hands against the trouser seams, arms against the body. A person who stands like that expects a command—about face!—that he will carry out zealously, or a reward—well done!—because he works so diligently. From childhood we are taught to stand like that, make ourselves small, and to pay attention in order to be liked: training for immaturity. I call it the "good child posture."

Here is an example of how easily and thoughtlessly we can violate the territory of our fellow beings. The boss comes into the office in a bad mood and, still caught up in his troubles, marches through the room with a mumbled "Mornin'," into his office without acknowledging his employees with a single glance. They are sour because he should at least have looked at them when he crossed their territory; this way, they have the feeling that he was demonstrating his superiority. Yet that was not at all what he had intended.

Every animal marks his territory with excrement, hair, rubbing against trees, with scent signals. The human being also "occupies" his territory with his body smell, the scent of perfume, with the odor of his brand of cigarettes or the smoke of his tobacco. More often, however, he marks it with objects that are recognizable as his possessions.

A passenger climbs into a plane and fills the seat to his left with his bag and the seat to his right with his newspaper. If someone comes and politely asks for the seat to be cleared, he is first given an intent stare: Can't you see my marks? But he insists, and the territory has to be vacated, whereupon the intruder is

Marking Territory

This gesture is not only casual and affectionate, it is also possessive.

conspicuously punished. The marker absently opens his paper and does not acknowledge him with another glance—he is a nonperson. If we move into a hotel room, we first unpack our things and mark our territory: clothes into the closet, reading material onto the table, shoes next to the door, toiletry articles into the bathroom.

In families the problem is greater because two or more have to share the same territory. The wife tidies her husband's things away in the morning and contentedly observes the signals of her neatness: She has taken possession of the territory again. He comes home, throws his jacket over the back of the chair

A usually unconscious but unmistakable gesture: What's under my hand is mine!

over here, puts his attaché case on the table over there, and his glasses next to the armchair: He is marking his territory. The wife is upset about the mess—after she had cleaned everything up so beautifully. But the argument is not about tidiness, it is about territorial rights. Order is reestablished when each of his territorial marking signs is in the place allocated to it. The jacket belongs on its hook, the attaché case next to the writing desk, the glasses in his reading corner.

Children scatter their toys throughout the apartment, preferably in the living room, where they do not belong. They are leaving their marks. And the mother picks the toys up, takes them back to the child's room where they do belong. The daughter's room is in a wonderful mess. While she is away, her mother tidies it up. Ingratitude is the way of the world: You've got no right to be in my room. A row ensues. Territorial rights and marking have been violated. What is important is that contrary signals always follow each other—in other words, a tidy daughter is reacting to an untidy mother.

We divide up unfamiliar or neutral territory equally. For instance a table in a cafe: Half belongs to me, the other half to the other person. If I lay something down, I take care that I do not cross this boundary. If the menu is lying on my side of the table, I pick it up as a matter of course; if it is in his half: May I? If I am engrossed in my newspaper and without thinking push away my plate so that it invades his territory, I notice in passing that it irritates him, and I withdraw. Every invasion of the other's territory is a challenge: He instinctively cuts himself off. The same happens at the conference table. If I push my papers under my business partner's nose, I irritate him, because I claim too much space. He withdraws, and communication becomes tough.

A young man applies for a job and from the outset wants to show that he is quite active and energetic. He comes in and says: "Good morning, my name is . . ." and rushes up to us, his hand outstretched. Reaction: Just a minute, not so fast, the man does not properly respect his boundaries and our zone, he will not subordinate himself easily; is he really that ambitious? His prospective colleagues instantly sense the competition and are on their guard; a reserved boss is likely to feel he is obtrusive, a sales manager considers him to be a very cocky salesman. But the young man probably did not have any of this in mind, he just wanted to show his willingness—and thereby violated the boundaries we have marked around us.

The moment his territorial rights are taken away, every person feels irritated: No one can eliminate this instinctive reaction. He may have come to terms with his subordination and accepted the dominance of others, but at the same time he still retains a feeling for his own territorial rights. Thus tensions and disputes can arise due to territorial conflicts even though we are not conscious of the cause.

In public and at work we are often forced to limit our territorial claims and come to terms with confined spatial conditions. This causes stress and overcrowding that repeatedly lead to aggressive outbreaks. In the formerly highly extolled open-plan offices, partitions between the individual working places or groups have again been installed, and thus the working atmosphere and performance have improved: Each person's space is marked again, his territory closed off from the others. At the assembly line there are always territorial clashes. The working places are too close together, the belt runs a little too fast, and instantly one is under territorial pressure, encroaches into one's neighbour's space, squabbles over trifles. Breaks are necessary in order to avoid such conflicts because of increasing

A person who leans across the table like this violates the other's territory.

fatigue, and to provide a chance to reduce the existing overcrowding.

It is a matter of course for us that we have to respect the territory of a stronger, superior person. The senior clerk knocks at the door; the secretary waits for the green light or the end of a telephone conversation or an inviting gesture, before she enters the boss' office. But what about the reverse situation? Does the director also respect his secretary's territory, or does he invade it without notice because, after all, he pays her, and she is dependent on him? If he does, he will not find her to be a very willing employee because she, too, lays claim to her territorial rights. A battle for status will now develop until the correctly graduated signals of their respective ranks have been properly established. The boss is hardly likely to knock on the door of his own outer office—that is too much trouble, a waste of time, and beneath his status. But he can draw attention to himself by clearing his throat, walking with loud steps, by pausing when he opens the door before he enters; or else he can always keep the

The secretary's dominant hand movement promptly triggers a disapproving sidelong glance from the boss.

door slightly ajar. In any event, some sign of warning must be given so that his employee can keep her self-respect and feel secure in her domain, be ready for his entry and have a chance to regain her composure if she is in the middle of cleaning out a desk drawer or blowing her nose.

Usually there is a reason for this visit: There is some work to be dealt with, some correspondence to be attended to. Does an understanding boss slam his papers down on the desk? By no means! The desk is her desk, its tidiness marks her territory, and every abrupt intrusion is like an invasion, an aggression, and it generates opposition, resistance, antifeelings. He is more likely to place the papers on the spot she allots, after exchanging glances of acknowledgment, or else hand them to her with an explanation.

Every visit, whether to the next room, the office, or a home, is penetration into unfamiliar territory. In the private sphere this often causes problems because close relatives and good friends often believe that they really can do whatever they

Anyone who lets a memorandum flutter down on a secretary's work area in this way grossly violates her territorial rights.

The forefinger pecks down on the secretary's shoulder like an eagle's beak; her defensive flinching from it is instinctive.

Such dominant instructions inevitably arouse uneasiness and antagonism.

Pointing something out with an open hand receives an open answer.

like, really can behave as if they were at home. The mother-in-law believes that her son (still) belongs to her territory, but the daughter-in-law believes the same, with greater right; or the helpful grandma moves around in the kitchen as if it were her own . . . and after one or two days of such clashes a spectacular family quarrel flares up. Usually the dear relatives do not understand it at all, and feel personally offended, rejected emotionally. Yet they have merely exceeded their territorial rights, and this could have been avoided with a little consideration and tact.

An Englishwoman once told me about an American guest whom she liked very much, but who annoyed her because without asking, he quite freely helped himself to anything in her refrigerator. When she visited him, he told her that she should simply get something from the refrigerator if she were thirsty, as is the custom in America. She did not want to do so, because it was counter to her territorial feeling. We therefore also have to bear in mind that territorial rights are interpreted differently according to the habits of various cultural groups.

A friendly and open greeting, yet the emotion hand does not participate.

An outgoing welcome to the visitor and an inviting movement of the emotion hand receive him as a friend.

The way someone receives us when we enter his territory also signals to what extent he accepts us. The relationship that he will permit is in direct proportion to the spatial distance he would like to preserve. I knock loudly on my boss's office door, get no answer, and am disconcerted, because he is making me wait: Acknowledgment has been refused. Fine, perhaps he is busy. Finally I hear: "Come in." I open the door and instantly the director leaps up behind his desk: "What is it?" I have not even crossed the threshold, and all I can say is: Yes, no, I'm disturbing you, excuse me, goodbye. Shot down with a cool stare. Or, after being invited in, I take two steps into the room, the man looks up expectantly and says: "What is it?" He is signalling: Be brief, I don't have much time. He can also let me get as far as the middle of the room, or even up to his desk. The fact that he continues to sit or very briefly raises his body, combined with the look and question, still means: Be brief. But this, if possible, would make me feel even more uncomfortable, because the farther I have to walk, the longer is my escape route. By the time I am finally standing in front of his desk, my

From behind the desk, the open and polite invitation to take a seat signals: I am receiving you in my official capacity.

Hands held back indicate: I will not act until you give me the appropriate impulses.

security is gone and my courage has disappeared.

If the person being visited, the "territorial master," wishes to avoid this uneasiness and receive his visitor in a friendly way, then he at least gets up, or he comes to meet him. How far he is prepared to "come to meet him" in his own territory is once again a clear signal. If he merely gets up between his chair and desk, he stays in his official capacity: The objects between which he moves are the signs of his position and function, to which he clings. If he leaves this protection and steps next to his desk, he is being a little more personal. If he goes right to the middle of the room toward his visitor, he is prepared to carry on a companionable conversation on an equal level; probably both of them will then turn together toward the desk. If he likes the visitor, or the visitor is his superior or seems important to him, then he is sure to hurry to meet him at the door and accompany him into his room. An important visitor does not intrude into territory: He is granted protection and escort in unfamiliar territory. He is received at the boundary. We are familiar with these subtle distinctions from the rules of international protocol. They are nothing more than highly political ritualizations of natural territorial behaviour.

But here, too, the saying "other countries, other customs" applies. In Arabic countries, it is the greatest insult to make someone wait at the door, even if one already has another visitor. This extensive hospitality probably arose from the harsh conditions of desert life: One does not leave the visitor standing in the blazing sun, one opens one's tent to him and quenches his thirst. This then leads to further Arab customs. For example, even under one's own roof guests are permitted to separate off in small groups and whisper in each other's ears—after all, they are merely showing that they do not want to disturb their host. In this country that would be considered rude, just as on the other hand an Arab would consider it improper if we did not invite him in immediately, yet would accept as a matter of course our continuing the conversation we had started after politely excusing ourselves to him.

There are still other associations connected with our territorial behaviour that are not evident at first sight. For instance, the car. No, not the car itself! A Porsche is much smaller than a Volkswagen bus, but the territorial claim of its owner is much greater than that of the VW bus driver. This depends less on the monetary value of the vehicle than on the space that it lays claim to when it is being driven. The Porsche is faster: In the same span of time it covers much more territory, and it needs a much longer braking distance. The driver measures the territory he is entitled to by such criteria, and woe betide anyone who intrudes into it without first giving polite notice. If he suddenly swerves in front of me or cuts across my lane, he has violated my territory, even if what he does is not dangerous. I react with fighting signals—flashing the lights, honking the horn, gestures, verbal insults—which belong in the encyclopedia of territorial behaviour.

Or time. The time that a person has is his possession, his territory. No one has the right to violate it. If he pushes us, he puts us under pressure, he comes too close. We "al-locate" our time and expect the time boundaries to be respected. A child becomes angry if we interrupt him in the middle of a game and give him a chore to do; he is more likely to accept our request if we have made it possible for him to plan his time appropriately beforehand. If someone wastes away our time with idle gossip, we not only say "You're driving me out of my mind!," we also say "You're wasting (depriving me of) my time!" He is taking away our territorial rights and claiming a period of time he is not entitled to.

And finally: our knowledge. Most people react impatiently and aggressively if someone intrudes into their sphere of knowledge without proper credentials. They will not tolerate him in territory for which he cannot prove himself, and push him back behind his boundaries. Nothing hurts them more than if their authority, their mastery of a field of knowledge, is not recognized; and they react aggressively if an amateur in the field lays claim to a subject in which he is not well versed, a subject that is terra nova for him, unfamiliar ground. In order to avoid such conflicts there are territorial demarcations: job titles, mastercraftsmen's certificates, academic titles, and hierarchical symbols.

Hierarchical Signals and Status Symbols

Every group creates its own social order. Its supporting structure is hierarchical order. In nature the strongest and most experienced is at the apex of the power pyramid, as long as he can assert himself against the pursuing forces. Their order of rank is determined by the measure of strength and superiority that they have displayed in their constant competition with one another. These battles of rivalry are observed and adhered to by all members of the group. Their outcome decides the confirmation of or change in status of the hierarchical order. Privileges and prerogatives are connected with this. In a horde of monkeys the leader is granted the most comfortable sleeping place in the tree that affords him the widest view to protect the others from enemies and himself from the others. He can also lay claim to the best food and any other sleeping place—any other's territory—but none of the others can claim his privileges. Through the respect he is shown (territory) the things he lays claim to become a symbol of his rank: status symbols.

People are not much different. But since they are particularly rational creatures and have a particularly complicated social order, a reversal of causes is also possible. In this case it is not their superiority and experience that gives value to the things they claim, but the possession of these things that gives the social rank; the symbol gives the status, however idiotic or obnoxious its owner may be. In the Middle Ages the child who held the imperial orb and sceptre in his hand was Imperator Mundi, acknowledged as an emperor; and the Borgia Pope, who presented himself with the papal crown and Roman crozier, was recognized as the highest worldly authority of all devout Christians. In a more modern context a worker knows that he can classify the hierarchy of the office types from the directors' floor according to the makes and models of their company cars. Value of symbol: power and comfort. And a company employee knows just as promptly where he should place a man in the hierarchy of management from the square footage of his office and the kind of plants in it—green or flowering, pots or vase, normal or hothouse. That is how refined and humane our customs are!

But the ground rules are somewhat simpler. One has to (1) be an adult in order to be recognized as a full member of society and be admitted into the competition for status, and (2) demonstrate through strength and stature in this competition what status one deserves, or is capable of earning.

Thus children enjoy special privileges in the social order because their bodily maturity, but also their right to have a say, are not yet pronounced. They are competitors neither in the fight for position nor in the rivalry of the sexes. Their behavioural signals arouse the protective instinct in adults and to a large extent permit them provocation, because they simultaneously block aggressive reactions. Small stature, smooth skin, and big round eyes characterize their outward appearance. Petite women like to take advantage of these attributes and the stimulating effect connected with them. They innocently look at everyone with big saucer-eyes, and thus cause a reaction block in a man as well as arousing his protective instinct, which is actually programmed for children. But men, too, "make

An insecure representative: His hands clutch the handle of his attaché case and hold it protectively in front of his body.

themselves small'' when they feel ill or miserable, want sympathy, and wish to be pampered.

Growing up is not only connected with bodily growth (size and strength), but also with the development of secondary sex characteristics. The breasts fill out, hair sprouts, and a beard adorns the face of a man. Emphasizing these signals also accentuates the adult status and is classed as showing off. Actually, grey hair, a wrinkled face, well-fed stomach, or a bald head should be coveted status symbols, because they are a sign of age and age means experience, wisdom, and property, and demands respect and reverence. Long ago and in noncivilized societies, this probably was so. But in the human social order the appreciation of natural signals has become a little confused—in the case of age one could also say we are again approaching primitive criteria. Because in Western society youthful appearance and vigorous energy possess the greatest value; as if one never passed the peak of life. One shaves one's beard, colours one's hair, keeps to a diet, uses cosmetics, and does everything just to seem young.

He behaves and presents his offer openly.

The status symbols of our society are:

- all kinds of titles
- political offices and professional positions
- possessions and property

Basically all these status symbols are equated with material values and social power. With money I can buy territory, and thus acquire power and my status. Intellect has only limited value, and should be connected with a title and provable influence, in other words, power. Yet material proof has the greatest effect: a spacious house, a large car, expensive clothing, valuable jewelry, a beautiful wife, a rich husband. Status symbols are orientation signs for others. They show the social rank and social differences; from them one can assess relative power balances, and correspondingly establish relations to each other. They can, however, also be used so obtrusively or brutally that with the appropriate difference in rank they can generate fear and inhibitions in the subordinate person, and human contact breaks off.

In this way he builds a wall between himself and his customer: What is he trying to hide?

There are also other ways in which status symbols can be misused. A house-to-house salesman may well earn so much that he can afford a crocodile-skin attaché case and a tailored suit from Chardin. But if he tries to sell Mrs. Smith the greatest mixer in the world in this attire, he is not likely to have any success. She feels the deal is shady, the guy dubious: With his symbols he carries excessive status around with him. Status symbols will be accepted as long as they are proportionate. Disproportionate status symbols always put people off if they seem presumptuous and ostentatious. Understatement is allowed; it is in its turn a status symbol of good manners, because even peculiarities of behaviour are suitable as symbols of social standing. Anyone who has money can buy an expensive suit, but one only learns good manners through years of practice and upbringing. In this way the social elite have adopted behavioural patterns from which one can instantly recognize which circle they belong to: They open the right doors better than any membership card. The nasal intonation of the Austrian aristocracy, the mess club tone of the Prussian officer caste, the upside-down fork of the English gentleman, the way one moves in a hunting party, or the banker with his dark blue suit—these are the things from which the insiders instantly recognize each other even in alien society, and unmask every imitator or interloper into their territory as an etiquette swindler.

For Instance: A Desk

The marks a person leaves around him and the way he behaves toward these objects tell us a lot about his status, his habits, relationships, and peculiarities. We enter an apartment and form a picture of its owner from it. We enter a study and can judge its owner from the position and state of the desk.

A large desk: Its owner likes to be comfortable and takes his work seriously. He considers his job to be important and tries to show this to others. If the size of the desk merely symbolizes status, we can recognize this from its style. A small desk: Its owner does little office work, or he does not take paperwork particularly seriously. But perhaps he is only unpretentious and a quick worker who gets things off his desk fast, and does much of his work on the telephone.

If the desk is standing in the middle of the room, it dominates the room—stable self-assurance.

If the desk is pushed into a corner, the owner likes to have visual control of the whole room from a safe position. He tends to want to know everything and has only limited trust in his partners.

A desk against the side wall shifts the axis of the room and avoids direct confrontation with the person entering, requires him to turn in that direction. But there is also a surprise element: The man behind it is hiding his dominance.

Naturally the position of the desk also depends on the lighting conditions in the room; but the extent to which it complies with them once again permits us to draw certain conclusions. Back to the light, facing the light, light from the side, artificial light—in which light does the owner show himself?!

A desk on which there is only one folder makes a clear statement. The man is concentrating on the matter now in hand, and expects it to be dealt with. Not until then can I broach a different subject.

Several folders in a neat row indicate that this person is keeping track of several matters and wants to handle them; he is also checking their interconnection and therefore wants to go through them in this order.

A desk piled high with folders in total disarray usually does not belong to a workaholic, but to a man whose work style is very erratic. His mind is already on the next or a totally different matter, and suddenly he brings that, too, over to the table, or catches up on something he had forgotten to mention before. One has to play along with this method, have patience, because he will not let the other person tie him down to one topic. Too many other ideas occur to him.

A desk without papers is the ultimate. The person behind it has an honorary seat, and administers representative functions, proclaims decisions, and plans grand projects. Others do the work.

The objects on the desk can also erect the Great Wall of China, behind which the owner has entrenched himself. Parallel to the edge of the desk, photographs, calendars, pens and pencils, the backs of books, and small sculptures erect a massive border fortification. The man allows no one to enter his territory and will always make his decisions alone, whatever we say. If he opens the wall and pushes a few things to the side, then he lets us get closer. But he would rather invite us over to a seating group for a cozy chat: Thus his habitual position remains untouched, and he commits himself to nothing. However, he makes his decisions on safe territory, behind the Great Wall of China.

And another thing. If the whole room makes an

aesthetically harmonious and elegant impression, its occupant appreciates a cultured conversation and sets great store by people who can talk on interesting matters. One should not come to him with shallow slogans and trivial arguments, but a good presentation and open explanation could win him over. By comparison, in a matter-of-fact, plain, and functionally furnished room, one can spare oneself this pleasantry. The master of this room works strictly economically and only wants to hear the crux of the matter.

Every company, every business, every organization has its hierarchical structure into which we are integrated according to our function. This rank also—but not exclusively—determines our social status. And lastly we also carry in us our own image of what we are, and would like to be. These three different status assignments stand side by side in three conceptions of the "I": this is how I am; this is how I think I am expected to be; this is how I would like to be. But naturally these "I" images blend in our behaviour. In rare, honest moments we really are ourselves. Usually we try to measure up to what others expect of us. And we almost never succeed in being how we would like to be. Nevertheless, these various forms and conceptions find expression also in the signals and symbols in which we show ourselves to the outside world. This can be very complicated, or easy to recognize. Here is one simple example.

On the desk we discover a miniature model of a golf club or we see a tennis trophy on the shelf. Our host placed it there with the quiet intention of saying: I may be the director, but I am also a sportsman and I have criteria other than those of hard business. If he really is a sportsman, and we subtly respond to this signal, we can count on fair negotiations. But if we notice that he merely shows off this "sportsmanship" as a status symbol, and the only movable thing on him is the keyring with the Porsche symbol, then, while it may be clever and flattering to treat him as if he really were a sportsman, we should not expect fair play from him. He would like to be what he is not.

Rituals

Each territory is surrounded by boundaries that mark it off from the territories of others and indicate one's own part within the mutual territory of one group, a larger community, or a whole nation. In their turn, these units are separated from others within the same order of magnitude by borderlines—for example, tribal boundaries, national boundaries, linguistic boundaries. Whatever is within my boundaries is my area and my property. Whoever moves within common boundaries identifies with the characteristics and objectives of the group in question and is accepted, or at least tolerated, by it. Anyone who lives outside these boundaries and approaches them is a potential intruder: He could have hostile intentions and violate our territory.

In order to remove this fear and make peaceful coexistence possible, people have developed a whole series of rituals with which they signal their friendly intentions when they approach alien territory. These rituals differ from culture group to culture group, yet one signal is common to all: the open hand.

Greetings

The open hand indicates that one is coming with peaceful intentions and is not carrying any weapons. In pictures of the culture of the Middle Ages, from the Occident through to the Far East, we are familiar with scenes in which armies lower their weapons in greeting, or the knights and samurai lay aside their swords when they enter a stranger's castle, and sit down to peaceful negotiations. In some primitive societies, when desert caravans meet they announce their peaceful intentions from afar with wild shouting and wild gesticulations, so that the others will not think that they are stealing into their territory. And the open hand signals the willingness to give.

With an open hand one presents to the host the gifts with which one pays honour to his status and requests his favour. This is customary in all cultures, and has been developed to such a specialized ritual in some Asiatic countries that the kind of present and the way it is handed over reveals exactly the social standing and the respect the participants have for each other.

In some Oriental and Eastern cultures one still kisses the ground on which the "big chief" is standing. The subject, but also the guest, demonstrates his submission in this way. The range of these gestures is like the evolutionary development of human customs toward democratic self-consciousness: from prostrating oneself on the ground and kissing feet, via kneeling and bowing, to nodding one's head and walking toward the other person, looking him straight in the eye.

In Russia and some Balkan countries one holds the other's arms with one's hands in greeting; symbolically and practically the hands are put out of action in this way. Then people kiss one another on the cheek in a brotherly way—but this, too, is done with fine nuances that depend on order of rank and esteem. The kiss can go straight past, into the air, cheek to cheek, it can be directly on the cheek, or even on the mouth. Among men this is a sign of great respect. In Latin countries, too, an embrace and a kiss on the cheek are a totally natural greeting ritual with which one expresses respect and liking.

In India and other Asiatic countries one hold one's palms together and slightly bows one's head in greeting: One dispenses with territorial fighting and shows humility. In Japan one holds one's hands flat against the upper thighs and one bends one's whole body forward; the depth of the bow depends on rank and respect. In the past this ritual was repeated often to show great reverence. Today, instead, people instantly exchange business cards, which also display title and position. It is as well to know that according to Japanese custom, this card is immediately read, and not put away. In most desert cultures the greeting usually takes the form of a brotherly embrace. This ceremony also has a very practical background: The wide clothing hides the shape of the body, but through the embrace one can discover any possible concealed weapons.

Handshakes

In contrast to the cultures of Asia and Africa, where direct eye contact when greeting someone is considered impolite and is either avoided or very quickly broken off, in the West steady eye contact is definitely a part of the ritual. People look in each other's eyes to show that they are capable of confrontation; yet through the other gestures of greeting they declare that they are renouncing territorial claims. Generally when doing this, one offers one's open hand.

Not so in America. There one sometimes only shows the open palm, raising one's arm slightly, and says the other's name: Hi, Jack! Hello, Mr. Miller. One has acknowledged the other and accepted him. The ritual has been complied with.

In England, too, one keeps one's distance, but in a very formal way. One does not step up close but stays far enough away so that sometimes it is simply uncomfortable to shake hands. My home is my castle: A gentleman prefers to avoid unnecessary contact. A hint at a bow is sufficient. One does not shake hands.

In German-speaking countries, direct eye contact and a strong handshake are almost a rule of etiquette. Any deviation puts the key to individual assessment in our hands. The pressure and the way one shakes hands indicate the measure of vitality, feeling, and objectivity that someone has or gives. An open and energetic greeting can be described like this: Two people walk toward each other with firm steps and stop at the right moment. This means that they have estimated the distance so precisely that without breaking step, or forcing the other to make any corrections, they both reach a position in which the distance is a little more than an arm's length: Neither can attack the other's body. With the body in an upright posture, the upper arm moves away from the chest and pushes the lower arm forward: The hands meet in the middle with an energetic grasp and are briefly shaken. If the upper arm does not free itself from the body, this indicates emotional inhibitions, and forces the other to come

We hold on to someone else's hands so that he will stay, because we need his attention.

closer to overcome the "holding back" by shortening the distance.

If, on the other hand, someone comes toward us with outstretched arm, he certainly gives the impression of "meeting us halfway." However, what he is really doing is blocking our free movement and forcing us to hold back. He often uses the space he has won to bow. When he straightens up and lets go of our hand, we realize that the distance is much greater than an arm's length: He has avoided getting closer and has kept his distance. The opposite happens when someone grasps our hand and draws it toward himself: He is pulling us in.

If the grip is too strong, it erects a barrier and makes one suspect that the other is covering up some insecurity. A limp hand along with a limp body posture indicates a lack of vitality, disinterest, or indifference. Observing the body posture is very important. Because if the other person is standing there straight and openly, in other words suggesting intensity and frankness, the limp hand merely states: Let's keep to the matter in hand,

There are reasons why the woman is critically rubbing her nose. While the man's greeting is friendly, his stiffly drawn back neck and locked elbows prevent a closer approach, and seem inappropriate.

and leave feelings out of it, I have no interest in closer personal contact.

If someone merely takes our hand between his fingers and thumb and then immediately breaks off skin contact, he is also signalling his aversion to starting a personal relationship. Another variation of this distaste for contact: Someone offers you his whole hand, but draws his palm in, so that you are left holding only the outer edge of his hand. There is no full contact with this hollow hand. A contrast to this is the fatherly greeting: The hand is taken between the two and surrounded by them. That is a discreet form of embrace that is meant to assure us of genuine affection.

If someone comes toward us with both hands outstretched, he usually arouses feelings of affection and assurance. But perhaps he merely wants to manipulate us? This is certainly the case if he grasps our hand with his and shakes it, while simultaneously taking hold of our elbow or upper arm with his other. This restricts our free movement; the other person can guide us in any direction with his left hand. By hinting at an embrace, he reveals his open feeling to us—but at the same time he would like to have our reactions under his control. This is the way that people who are loving but possessive behave.

Meals

Food is a basic need, the right to food a basic element of territorial right. I will drive off anyone who feeds on the fruits of my fields and labours in my territory without my consent, because he is robbing me of my fundamental needs. In the group, too, precise rules have been laid down through acquired or inherited rank and possessory titles, as to who has a right to which portions of the territory and the food that it produces. Favours are given out to subordinate members of the group by inviting them to meals, and the seating order at the table reflects the hierarchical succession. The person who sits at the head has the highest status, and the closer one sits to the foot, the lower is the social standing. The guest whom one wants to make especially welcome, the person whom one wishes to set apart for a particular reason, receives the place of honour at the head of the table, next to the man of the house.

All important events are celebrated with feasts: weddings, baptisms, birthdays, funerals, victories, fraternizations, and important visitors. No expense is spared, one displays what the territory has to offer; the status and reputation of the host demand it. Eating, too, is a status symbol and the ritualization of this procedure during the event is unmistakable. That applies down to everyday habits. Since eating is also enjoyable, and connected with pleasant sensations and happy feelings, the characteristics and relationships of people are revealed by it.

An invitation to lunch signals: We do not have much to do with one another personally, but we get on well, and would like that to continue. An invitation to dinner goes a step further: We want to get to know each other better, and for that I have time privately. If both marriage partners are included in this meeting, it also accepts the beginnings of closer relationships, and goes yet another step further: We do not have to meet exclusively for business reasons—maybe we can find personal contact?

Such nuances are also precisely registered in purely private, neighbourly relations. Three invitations to afternoon coffee and two for champagne breakfasts—even if the cakes are plentiful, and the champagne flows freely—are together not worth as much as two for dinner. If you do not believe this, just think of the careful considerations that went into compiling the list of invitations for your last summer evening party—or of how many people among all the obligatory ones you really want to invite. It is not just a matter of what one offers but when. Occasionally rituals are very precise forms of demonstrating liking.

On the other hand, from the manner in which I give the invitation I can demonstrate empathy and liking—even at the wrong time. Do I go to an elegant restaurant to impress my guest, or do I choose one that suits his taste or our mood? Exotic cuisine or a cozy atmosphere can be the deciding factor or, after exhausting hours at a conference, a bar or a wine cellar may be the right thing. However, one thing is certain, our guest will not judge what to think of us from the amount of the bill, but from the measure of understanding and harmony.

Hospitality is a very reliable means of communication—good or bad. We must not underestimate the small gestures. A cup of coffee, or would you prefer espresso? A glass of tea, perhaps with milk and sugar? A short drink, mineral water to go with it? Or a longer one? This invitation always relieves us of territorial restraint, and indicates our efforts to open up. You give, and he accepts. We come into contact with each other, and neither has compromised himself.

In our organism each part of the body has a function assigned to it. From the build of the bones and the joints, from the structure of muscles and tendons, from the nature of tissues and the nerves, we can recognize the characteristics that make the body able to deal with its special functions, through which it fulfills its role in the interaction of the whole body.

Roles are also assigned in social organization. Each individual receives self-affirmation and recognition to the degree to which he fulfills his functions and tasks. He assumes duties and receives rights for them that determine his status and position.

Every person changes his role several times during his life. He is a child, an adolescent, a lover, a marriage partner, parent, in-law, and grandparent. Each of these roles demands its own behaviour and own signals, the framework of which are the rights and duties set by social rules and expectations. He also has to play some of these roles simultaneously—as a husband he should not behave like a grandfather, and as a father he should not always play the experienced old man. This demands rather a lot of flexibility in the intimate circle alone.

But he also has a professional role to fulfill. As a worker or employee, soldier or civil servant, doctor or lawyer, manager or priest, bank president or politician, he not only assumes a function in public life, but also the behavioural pattern connected with the specific role: body behaviour, mimicry, language, and outward status symbols. Others not only expect him to fulfill his function well because he is granted his rights in the group and society for this, they also expect him to play his role well so that they can recognize him in it from specific behavioural signals. He, too, expects his role to be acknowledged and the rights connected with it to be accepted as a matter of course. This can only work if the role is identifiable by its specific behavioural signals and forms of expression.

We can only get our bearings from these outward signs, the character of a role. We expect propriety and determination from a military officer, respectability and cool sober-mindedness from a bank president, tolerance and compassion from a priest— and we want to see these role functions in their behaviour and performance. Otherwise they seem untrustworthy to us. In the same way, someone who signals a role he is not entitled to arouses suspicion: a swindler.

In order to fulfill these expectations, some identification of the person with his role is necessary, which is not always easy. One has to bring the inner world of the person into harmony with the outer world of the role. But contradictions can

Role Functions

A small correcting movement: I would like to please.

Relief from the restraint of convention: With a spontaneous movement the hand provides freedom.

Social etiquette: One makes oneself into the person one is meant to be.

arise between the "I" and the "should," between what one is, and what one would like to be, and the man one is expected to be. They do not have to result from excessive demands. They can also arise if someone believes he has to play a role differently than is generally expected, in other words, in his own way. Such conflicts can trigger frustrations, repressions and inhibitions, guilt feelings, and anxieties, and lead to unsatisfactory behaviour. But sometimes the role can be to blame if we rate it too highly and idealize it. Idealizing a role makes it rigid and inflexible, it makes itself independent, and leaves no room for the "I." Thus we find people becoming functional machines without individual feelings: The role has swallowed them up. They suppress the impulses of their "I" and forget how to deal with their feelings.

This is a particularly great danger because in our prestige-hungry, achievement-oriented society, the work function has absolute priority. The models of the professional role also colour private behaviour and relatively often cover up the demands of the private functions. Stress and exhaustion contribute to this. We are all familiar with the indignant family cry: "You're not in the office now!" or "Don't play the big boss!" These days it sounds wrong for someone to brag that he leaves the job back in his office. Shouldn't this really be a matter of course? Yet, in fact, many people still carry their office attitudes around with them at home like a shield, and hardly notice that by doing this they are erecting barriers and no longer fulfill their family function.

A bank manager's child does not need advice on investments, but rather a father who does not think twice about crawling under the table with him even when guests are present. And his wife needs a husband who is not worried about presenting a respectable appearance to his neighbours when he is fooling around in the garden with her and the children, who are pelting him with dirt. Otherwise the man can indeed retain his dignity as a distinguished businessman who commands respect, but lose his value as a father and a husband, the respect and love of his family. Because these functions demand different role behaviour from him.

It is a matter of playing the appropriate role in the right place, at the right time, and that is certainly not always the role "they" expect, but the role one's partner expects or needs. The wife is sure to be quite pleased when her husband acts not only like an attentive spouse, but also displays his superior professional position at a large party. But at lunch on Sunday, in the kitchen, she would prefer to have a cheerful head of the family, and on a beautiful summer evening, a romantic lover. The young employee in the office certainly respects his boss's professional qualities, but sometimes he simply needs fatherly advice. A friend appreciates a great pal and knows his qualities, but he can do without the advice of a successful know-it-all. When we play the various functions of our different roles, we only utilize and develop the abilities nature has given us. We have to bring them into harmony with our "I," that is right and important. But in our attempts at flexibility and dynamic development, we broaden this "I" and become what we could be: husband's wives, parents, friends, and colleagues.

However, our upbringing and the ground rules of society are not set up for this. They are occupied with behavioural patterns and regulations that are designed to fulfill expectations and to guarantee our function as a group. We hardly have a chance to discover and determine our own worth, but are conditioned to adjust our conception of our own value according to our usefulness to the community.

To begin with we hear from our parents whether we are good or bad children, then from teachers whether we are good or bad students. Then our employers judge whether we are any good and what we are worth. Officers and authorities decide whether we are good or undisciplined citizens. It is always others who make the decisions according to their own expectations, and that is why we have to fulfill them. Our self-assessment is set up to depend on their recognition, so we have to conform. We assume the duties demanded of us and subordinate ourselves so as to get our rights in return. So that our inner equilibrium does not go to the devil, we pretend that this is our own voluntary decision, and justify this rationalization with the conviction that without us the others could not manage at all. This apparently brings balance into the whole role distribution. I would like to illustrate this with a few scenes.

The husband comes home, throws his attaché case in a corner, drops into a chair still wearing his coat, and *she* is still nowhere to be seen. Finally she comes in: "I'm sorry, I was at the stove." She takes off his shoes.

"Don't pull so hard!"

"I'm sorry, forgive me." She puts the shoes and coat away, gets his slippers while he marches over to the armchair.

"Damn it, do you always have to leave your things in my chair?" He crabbily thrusts her knitting at her.

"I'm sorry, I just forgot it . . ."

"When's dinner going to be ready?"

"Right now, I was just about to bring it."

218

Grumble, grab for the newspaper, by then dinner is served.

"Is it good, d'you like it?"

Spooning, without looking up: "The soup's too hot."

This can go on for a whole evening: He will always find something to criticize, and this continues throughout the marriage.

But what happens if one day he hangs up the coat himself, puts away his shoes, lays aside the knitting, and finds the soup wonderful? For her it would be a catastrophe, because her self-esteem would collapse. She sacrificed herself, did everything for him, was always there for him—and now none of that is valid any more. She was firmly convinced that he could not live without her, and now he can, after all. He removed the dependence with which she was compensated for her submission, and thus destroyed her inner equilibrium.

Naturally it always takes two to play the game. She could, of course, immediately refuse to be submissive and set

A warning glance, a commanding hand gesture: You had better obey!

other ground rules. In that case he could not play the house tyrant. We cannot always put the blame on others, since we play along with their game. If I fulfill their expectations, it is my reaction, and not their fault. And if I do not fulfill them, it becomes their problem, and not mine. Because then the others must check whether they have set the right expectations, and whether I am actually willing to comply with them. In other words, decisions based on a free feeling of one's own worth are uncomfortable for others, because then it is difficult to fit people into a plan and make use of them. It is easier to limit their ability to decide through strict norms and expectations from the very beginning and to cultivate their sense of duty. Then, if they are neglectful of their duties, their bad conscience will bring them back onto the right track. That is the ritual of social blackmail.

True social maturity would mean that one first imparts to people the consciousness of their own worth and their individual abilities. People should be sure of themselves before tackling a task. That way, their performance at that task will not

A suggestive glance, a pacifying gesture: Surely you can see that?

220

affect their self-esteem. They will know that some tasks suit their abilities better than others, and that they are not there simply to accept and fulfill the arbitrary or unreasonable expectations of others. It is not until I take on a responsibility, conscious of my own worth and having calmly assessed my abilities and strengths, that I no longer simply fulfill expectations. Nor do I then fall apart if I do not succeed. But when someone undertakes such a task because of pressure or ambition, in order to please others and justify their expectations, it leads to problems. Self-esteem can be bruised if the person fails at the task, and future tasks can be hindered by resultant feelings of inferiority.

Of course I also realize that there is an interdependence between myself and the other person; and in order for people to coexist, we must be able to depend upon one another within certain parameters, so as not to be disappointed in our expectations. There are enough rules that set this behavioural framework, and some that limit it too much. Because for the very reason that this dependence is mutual and applies to everyone, it is useful to each individual, and to the community as a whole, if this "sphere of expectations" is not set too narrowly. False expectations, or expectations that have been set too high, can overtax and overburden the individual, and result in reduced self-confidence, psychosomatic illnesses, and drop in performance. And the person who sets them not only suffers disappointment, but also inevitably falls victim to faulty planning, which reduces his own productivity. In the end it turns out that everyone's developmental abilities have been mutually hampered and harmed under the pressure of expectations.

By the way, things are no different in the sphere of politics and ideology. A person who constantly repeats the opinions of Marx, Popper, Keynes, or Freedman, admittedly fulfills the expectations of the party or group whose recognition he craves. But he will hardly qualify as a mature citizen. To do so he would have to examine critically all ideas, being fully conscious of his own worth and having assessed his own abilities and experiences, then adopt ideas and enrich them with his own colour through his own thoughts and reflections. One should only regurgitate something that one has properly digested.

The Clothing Codex

We have already recognized a certain kind of clothing as a status symbol. Here we have to look at it once more in its significance as a role signal. In the way one dresses, or in what one wears for which occasion, one identifies with a specific group or a specific event, one emphasises one's role. This is what happens with the dark blue suit at a wedding (silver tie) or a funeral (black tie). At grand festivities and receptions, etiquette prescribes tails or dinner jacket. A person who cannot appear dressed like this disappoints the expectations and fails in his role, or stays at home. In the counterculture, one ostentatiously turns against middle-class dress codes and develops one's own. Whether it is the punks or the poppers or the rockers, a person who does not comply with the ritual of their attire does not belong to the group. Students wear jeans and patterned shirts, sheep's wool, Grandma's clothes, not only because it is comfortable but also to demonstrate a certain casual attitude. A person who runs around in a suit and tie at a university is either a professor, an employee, or an overambitious person who wants to clamber upward fast.

In the past, the role character of clothing was even more marked and was easier to recognize. In the Middle Ages there were strict clothing regulations that determined what was in keeping with one's standing right down to the number of buttons and the value of the braid, and that meted out punishment if, for instance, a simple citizen contravened these regulations by putting on clothing that was worthy only of a nobleman. From the clothing one could see to which craftsmen's guild a person belonged, and whether he was a journeyman or a master. These clear recognition signals disappeared when the strict social order dissolved, and modern development no longer permitted social differences to stand out. Uniform clothing has held its own or prevailed only in a few professional groups in which it was necessary as a role signal and desirable as a status symbol: the uniform of soldiers or the police, clerical robes, the habits of religious orders, the white coats of doctors and nurses, the uniforms of employees of the post office, railways, and people working for other public transport institutions, the livery of hotel personnel, and an elegant waiter's tails and black tie. If we look very closely we can, of course, recognize role insignia in a whole series of professions, particularly old ones: a butcher's or blacksmith's apron, a cook's hat, and the carpenter's cap. . . .

But what is more important is that in its turn modern society has developed its own conventions that link particular roles with particular clothing features, and the way one wears one's clothes is connected with certain status symbols. The workers' overalls admittedly stay in the locker in the factory, and even the office employee's grey flannel suit had yielded in its turn to the fashionable easing up influenced by casual leisure clothing. But an administrative assistant without a tie—unacceptable. The higher one climbs in the hierarchical pyramid, the more imperative the conventions become, and the more can be read into the deviations that a role-bearer allows himself from the norm of his role behaviour. Bankers, businessmen, and personalities in public life who really do have power and influence wear dark blue or dark grey suits. A pinstripe is good, and emphasizes the conservative, traditional element: the reserved behaviour of the English upper class, or the refined inconspicuousness of the French financial aristocracy—a class distinction, suitable for leading bankers, members of the board, and presidents who have already established their capabilities or capital resources and now administer them from an elevated position. It would be better for sharp senior personnel to avoid the pinstripe: In their case it is more likely to signal a "would like to be" attitude. Zealous climbers also have to be careful with dark blue and pinstripes: Wearing these unmasks them as role players and invites manipulation. Such people are ready to show any amount of servility for an appropriate number of stroking units from above or admiration from below. Such misdemeanors are no longer looked down on by middle management, but in the end effect they block the entrance to the very top floor. Up there a closed circle rules with its own criteria for co-opting people, in which integrity and tradition once again play an important role.

On top management levels, among the directors and executive board, comfort and sportiness are also permissible. English tweed and casually worn sportcoats are allowed on the right occasion. A person who is clothed comfortably also has a comfortable life: He values more pleasant surroundings and sets great store by good service. The sportiness need not be genuine. Golf and horseback-riding are good, the correct club colours in one's tie, and a discreet club badge are more important than athletic ambitions. The comfort must not be trendily stylish—that would seem slightly unreliable. As far as women are concerned—if they are allowed to advance into the higher ranks for reasons other than visiting or show—their clothing and jewelry also may not reveal too much fashionable style. Timeless elegance is preferred; especially suits or a skirt, blouse, and jacket. In other words, clothing in which the lords of creation can still see their masculine dominance.

Taste can also serve as a signal. Advertisers, interior decorators, and architects love striking patterns and unusual ideas.

The weak point is in down below, where the feet are.

We look at ourselves in the mirror, and our clothes are just right—except for our feet. Those are very sensitive parts of our body. We are on our feet all day long, literally or figuratively. This is where the reflex zones of all organs and parts of the body end. From here the energy streams upward in the flight of our thoughts and back down to the ground on which we stand. The feet are a very private part of our body. They want to—have to—be comfortable, because otherwise we are cut off from our own roots. But we have to encase them in shoes, and they often form a contradiction to the rest of our clothing. Above we signal: This is the way I would like to be. Below we show: This is what I am.

Old, worn shoes actually seldom indicate miserliness. They are more likely to indicate faithfulness, loyalty, dependence on old habits. Their owner finds it difficult to part with familiar relationships, and will put up with a lot just to avoid change. The thought of a fresh start terrifies him, because new shoes pinch, and the old ones will do for a while yet. Quite often one sees wide, comfortable shoes beneath a very correct (in fact, rather formal) suit. The contradiction is clearly visible. Admittedly the man will zealously fulfill the expectations of his role, but basically it is all too complicated and costly as far as he is concerned. So let's do what is expected, but for heaven's sake don't let's make it too complicated, and let's deal with it in as comfortable a way as possible; anyway I'm happiest when I'm back home again. But don't take me for a fool because of this. Fashionable shoes speak for themselves. Being fashionable at all costs, today counts, yesterday is gone, we'll talk about tomorrow later, and I don't care any more for comfort than I do for quiet contentment. Thin, supple shoes are exquisite and expensive, and comfortable, and elegant. For such quality of life the man is prepared to invest some effort and take some trouble. Such shoes last only if one takes good care of them. Sturdy shoes with thick soles indicate a stable master of the house. He will put in a lot of effort, but he has to get something long-lasting in return.

Epilogue

After we have gone from protein molecules to large social organizations, from instincts to rituals, from the head to the feet, I would like to close my remarks about body language as an expression of human behaviour with a warning.

Never trust body language, because human nature is full of guile and self-deception. It was during a guest appearance in London that I finally realized this. A very important, very eminent critic was sitting in the front row. I was moving around on the stage. He grimaced and stared at me with an incredibly sour expression. I made every effort to surpass myself. He did not move a muscle. The "sour apple expression" seemed to be frozen on his face. It was enough to drive one to despair. After the performance, the man came to my dressing room. He still had the same sour expression. He stepped up to me shaking his head, grasped my hand, shook it, and said: "Unbelievable . . . truly unbelievable!"

I have not written this book to set forth my observations and research as new discoveries. On the contrary. I would like to stimulate your awareness of, and sensitivity to, known and documented signals of body language, whose meaning has been lost through the habituation of everyday routine. If you recognize these signs in yourself and in others again, and use them as a means for better understanding, then these pages have fulfilled my hopes.